*Henri Cartier-Bresson is recognized as
one of the great photographers of all time.
He is known throughout the world
for his photographic essays on the death
of Gandhi, the fall of Shanghai,
and the independence of Indonesia.*

*He has won three Overseas Press
Club Awards. One-man shows of his
work have been presented at the
Louvre and the Museum of Modern Art.
His numerous books include*
THE DECISIVE MOMENT, THE EUROPEANS
and THE PEOPLE OF MOSCOW.

CHINA *is one of Henri Cartier-Bresson's
most brilliant achievements—the stark,
revealing study of the people and
places of a great land ravaged by war,
famine, flood and tyranny*

Thousands of school and university students jam the area around Peking's Tien An Men Palace to hear anti-American speeches by their leaders. The brightly colored banners carry slogans protesting the presence of American troops in Lebanon.

CHINA

PHOTOGRAPHED BY
HENRI CARTIER-BRESSON

TEXT BY HENRI CARTIER-BRESSON
AND BARBARA BRAKELEY MILLER

A GALLERY EDITION / BANTAM BOOKS / NEW YORK

CHINA / A Bantam Gallery Edition / Published April
1964. Library of Congress Catalog Card Number: 63-8929.
All rights reserved. © Copyright, 1964, by Henri Cartier-
Bresson. Published simultaneously in the United States
and Canada. Bantam Books are published by Bantam
Books, Inc. Its trade-mark, consisting of the words "Bantam
Books" and the portrayal of a bantam, is registered in the
United States Patent Office and in other countries. Marca
Registrada. Printed in the United States of America.
Bantam Books, Inc., 271 Madison Ave., New York 16, N. Y.

CHINA

PART ONE
CHINA IN TRANSITION

PART TWO
A DECADE LATER

PART THREE
CHINA IN HER 4000 YEARS

PREFACE

To the eighteenth-century French philosopher and writer, Jean Jacques Rousseau, the Chinese were the quintessence of wisdom and moderation, the incarnation of universal reason. By the next century, the Occident thought of them in terms of Confucius's sayings, and in the twentieth century, yet another image appeared, this time, on the movie screens. It was the Machiavellian and translucently polite Chinese who manipulated destinies through the powerful Secret Societies. From the novelists of the same period, we have the straw-hatted peasant, happy in his simplicity in the rice paddies.

Then, almost overnight, another version appeared. The picturesque had turned political. The label now read "Communist." But the nature of the Chinese was, and is, as enigmatic as ever, a situation accentuated by the fact that few Westerners, and almost no Americans, have visited the People's Republic since its inauguration in October 1949. As a French free-lance photographer, I had the good fortune to be present during the strife-ridden transition period between the two Chinas. During my eleven months as war correspondent, I witnessed the last five months, and defeat, of Generalissimo Chiang Kai-shek's Kuomintang or Nationalist Government and the first six months of Chairman Mao Tse-tung's Communist regime. I returned ten years later to see how 650,000,000 people were living under the red flag with the five yellow stars. These two photographic reportages, both of war and peace, were destined for publication in *Life, Paris Match,* and other major European magazines.

In answer to the inevitable question, What are the Chinese now like? I would answer they are 3000 years old —plus thirteen. I might also describe them as "frustrated": the frustration of all peoples who try to tear away the tentacles of those thousands of years in order to compete in the modern age. Their Chinese pride forces them to avenge the humiliations which had been inflicted by the West for almost one hundred years. But, since my return in 1959, events have proved the program of China's Communist leaders to have been too ambitious (see chronological history). Their Five-Year Plans, drawn at times more from blueprints than reality, were harassed by natural calamities and the exhaustion of the population in that frenetic rush to achieve success at any cost.

I have frequently felt that unspoken desire of people to see a statement of approval or disapproval when they look at my photographs of Communist China. The new China is composed of many fascinating ingredients. As a wandering "street photographer" I had the opportunity to savor a great many of them through the lens of my camera. I present them to you in this book not as political commentary, but as visual observations of a nation of over half a billion people, one-fourth of the world's population, and multiplying rapidly, who are in full evolution, with all the resulting upheavals. Since one can neither reverse this direction nor place China outside the walls of the world, it is perhaps preferable to understand the facts of its existence.

Henri Cartier-Bresson

CHINA IN TRANSITION

In December of 1948, I was photographing in Burma when *Life* gave me the assignment to cover the civil war in China. I was to start in Peiping, already under heavy attack by the "People's Liberation Army."

(When Cartier-Bresson landed in Peiping, now called Peking, Chiang Kai-shek's Kuomintang Army was losing heavily all along the front. In two months, it had been defeated in four major battles which netted the Communists 18 full divisions, 9 brigades, and 15 regiments. Morale was low and many Kuomintang soldiers were defecting to the other side. By early December, Manchuria was in Communist hands, and General Lin Piao had rushed his men to the outskirts of Peiping before the Kuomintang could recover from their losses in the north.)

Yet, inside the ancient walls of Peiping, the daily routine remained fixed in time, a peaceful island within war-torn China.

As usual, the gentlemen of the city arrived promptly at 9 A.M. at their favorite teahouses. Some carried birds, some crickets. They hung their cages from hooks in the ceiling, or settled them next to their cup of tea. A venerable gentleman held his bird attached by a string to a stick. Another tickled his cricket with a long horsehair until it burst into chirping song. A third covered his bird cage with a curtain to keep the warmth in and the street noises out. My teahouse was silent: its clients meditating rather than talking. A sign on the wall read: *"Track down the unstable elements,"* a euphemism for Communists.

Out in the streets, public bulletin boards, erected by local newspapers, made war news available to strolling Peiping citizens. People crowded around them. Judging from their dispassionate attitudes, they might have been looking at real estate ads or want ad notices. Everyone must have been aware that the Kuomintang government was losing rapidly in the face of the determined People's Liberation Army. But the course of history would not interrupt their lives. The calm detachment, still so great a Chinese virtue, was being maintained on the eve of the downfall of their city.

Nevertheless, there were evidences of urgency. A truck rolled by carrying a banner and a band. The loudspeaker blared out an appeal for 10,000 volunteers to defend Peiping. General conscription would be put into effect in any case, and these volunteers were promised special privileges if they came forward immediately. The appeal netted 14 volunteers—and 10,000 conscripts. The volunteers were presented with gifts by the garrison commander for volunteering "without claiming money or honors." The conscripts lined up quietly in a palace courtyard. Resigned, impassive, they had no illusions about their capacity to change history's course. Warned by the disturbance, relatives rushed to the scene to see if one of theirs was in the ranks. In these last days of Kuomintang control, the youngsters were called up so fast, they had no time to notify their parents. The general in command of them, Fu Tso Yi, highly respected by the American delegation, crossed to the Communist side, shortly after the fall of Peking, and now heads the Ministry of Water Conservation.

The People's Liberation Army was at the walls of Peking. Kuomintang troops were disappearing southward. The Communists had won North China. At the airfield, I managed to squeeze into the last plane leaving the besieged city. We taxied down the runway, then rose suddenly straight up toward the sky like a corkscrew, when the pilot saw Communist soldiers pouring onto the field. We landed in Shanghai, still held by Chiang Kai-shek's government, where I continued my assignment.

In contrast to tranquil Peking, this cosmopolitan port, long a prosperous center of foreign trade, was in the grip of an intense frenetic activity. In the streets and along the quays, the people rushed and pushed, as though manipulated by invisible, but conflicting and disorganizing, forces. On Soochow Creek, the slow-drifting sampans were jammed against each other, moving aimlessly like thick ice floes. Already overcrowded, Shanghai now had the added burden of refugees, people and sampans, fleeing the fighting down on the Yangtze River. The air echoed with shrill cries as the traffic jams frustrated even the most resigned. But blows were never dealt. Wrong is on the side of he who strikes first, according to Chinese ways.

A part of the river traffic was in coffins, occupied and

unoccupied. In the recent strife-ridden months, many practical souls, after watching the value of the yuan dribble away, decided to invest in luxurious coffins. But, due to the war and the lack of transportation, they and their coffins were piling up on the dock. Death, in Shanghai as on the battlefront, was simply a part of the daily life. Only the stevedores seemed to mourn these stranded coffins as they unloaded them from trucks to the tune of a mournful singsong. But such plaintive chanting was heard whenever these men carried heavy loads.

On the Bund, Shanghai's once prosperous quay, a body of a child had been pushed out of the way against a wall, by the side of a dead cat. The child was still wearing the traditional quilted red coat. No one spared him a glance. In the past hundred years, war, rebellion, epidemics, famines and floods had taken a toll of almost a billion Chinese. In the twenty years of Kuomintang rule, millions had died. A discarded child, dead or alive, was a common sight in this city whose population of 5,000,000 had been drastically inflated by thousands upon thousands of refugees who settled like crows in any available space, exhausted and famished. (In 1961 the population of Shanghai was reputed to be 7,100,000.) As stevedores carried bales of cotton from sampans to carts, scores of hands flashed out to rip away hunks of this precious staple commodity. In the cold of this war-torn December, every scrap helped to pad out the worn quilted coats. Women and children scurried across the quay grasping pieces of coal, sticks of wood, a few grains of rice or wheat, the daily necessities that had become luxuries. Each day at dawn, these crowds arrived and waited, prepared to steal before the police would stop them: vigilant eyes and hands, too numerous and too desperate for the weary authorities.

On Christmas Eve, the gold yuan dropped from 68 to 93 to the dollar. The Kuomintang suspended all sales of gold and silver for the day. The next day the authorities announced that they would distribute 40 grams of gold per person and the Gold Rush was on. Hordes of people queued up before the doors of the banks on the Bund, some waiting for 24 hours to exchange their paper money. As pressure built up, the line looked like a human accordion, squeezed in and out by invisible hands. Given the panic and hysteria, the police acted with leniency. To control and prevent riots, they only splashed cold dirty water from puddles or prodded the people with the rods used to clean their guns. Even as I watched, the gold-hungry crowd grew into such a mass that the police were immobilized, their arms pinned to their sides. I felt hands searching through my pockets. I smiled, and a man smiled back, nodding his head and producing the only thing he had discovered, a bit of pencil. He returned it to me graciously.

During the month of December, Chinese Buddhists and Taoists organized special pilgrimages to pray for peace. While Nationalists and Communists killed each other on the Yangtze River, processions of peasants and priests paraded from temple to temple in the ancient city of Hangchow. The memories hovering over this city reflected the long brilliant history of China. The Emperor Yu, semi-legendary founder of the nation's first dynasty, the Hsia, was said to have stayed there about 2200 B.C. The Sung Emperors made it their capital in 1138 A.D. Then the Mongol hordes under the all-conquering Genghis Khan captured it in 1278. When Marco Polo served in the Mongol Court, he noted down the beauties of Hangchow which somehow had survived the sacking and looting that inevitably accompanied the fall and rise of the successive dynasties. Even the Japanese had passed time here, from 1937-45. Now, China's future was again being solved in warfare, the faithful added peace to their traditional prayers for good harvests, good health, and much wealth. A procession of Buddhist pilgrims paraded through the town preceded by green and white banners. The pilgrims were young men whose bare chests were studded with silver needles. They carried beautifully carved sticks held between outstretched arms. Then came two men walking within a bamboo frame from which were suspended images of the Buddha. These men also had silver needles covering their chests. When the procession halted in the courtyard of the temple, some entered to offer prayers and incense, while others remained in the courtyard sticking gold needles with ritual gestures into their flesh. In time of crisis, the Chinese seemed to find considerable comfort in gold and silver whether in the Treasury or in their skin—a curious contrast to the wretched women scrabbling in the dust for a few grains of rice or a handful of cotton.

While following the pilgrimages in Hangchow, I heard that the situation was rapidly deteriorating for the Kuomintang government. Chiang Kai-shek had already left his capital of Nanking, and by so doing had stepped down from his position as president. Now, in the middle of April, the battlefront was rapidly approaching Nanking. The Communists had concentrated 1,000,000 soldiers of the People's Liberation Army along the 600-mile front skirting the north bank of the Yangtze River.

But, when I arrived in the capital, war seemed to be at a standstill. There was an emptiness in this city, a quiet that denied the existence of strife. The long avenues and vast concrete government ministries seemed shabbier than ever, but then they never had looked new even though recently built by the Nationalist regime. In this dismal capital, one felt the feeble pulse of the Kuomintang in its death throes, a pulse that had been steadily weakening under the strain of the Civil War its leaders insisted on fighting. In true Chinese fashion, the present dilemma had come about because those in authority were more concerned with conforming to the rules of the game than in seeking the meaning behind it. The old rule of "saving face" had been observed. In China, face-saving is not applied like a stiff mask of status quo but as a dignified exit out of a deadlocked situation. However, in actual fact, there was no longer any face to save. The authorities were more occupied in fleeing with their faces intact.

Face-saving is also of little consequence to those facing hunger, with no roof over their heads. From 5000 to 10,000 refugees had fled before the Communist forces, across the Yangtze River, to the supposed shelter of the Nationalist forces in Nanking. But the collapse of the government money made it impossible for them to earn enough to eat, let alone to sleep in a bed. So the thousands returned to the banks of the Yangtze to try to persuade the ferryman to return to the other side, and the Communist lines. One of the ferry boats lay tied to the dock, immobilized by lack of coal. The refugees crowded onto the wharf, crushed between ropes and anchors and barrels, waiting for hours with blank resignation for coal to arrive. No one ventured to say when it would. Once in a while, a woman, voice shrill in desperation, would rush forward to shove her last bits of money into the face of a sampan owner, pleading for passage.

In contrast, the Tsung Yang Lu Park, with its lotus ponds and little islands, was as tranquil as ever. A few soldiers wandered bored and aimless, with the front but a few miles away! One, even more isolated from historical events, played a delicate air on a flute.

The Legislative Yuan was in session during these last tense days. Chiang Kai-shek had summoned a number of the old war lords to Nanking in a show of loyalty to his government, among them: Marshall Yen Si Chan who had been behind or in front of every political crisis in the past half century, and General Ma Hung Kuei, governor of Ningsia, famed for his Moslem soldiers and his taste for ice cream as served by his young wife!

Rumors in the beginning of April were so rampant that you had only to cock your ear in the street to hear a dozen or so. The Nationalist officials were in Peking talking cease-fire arrangements with their Communist opposite numbers. The cease fire was rumored to be in effect, then not to be, and so it went. When the chief of the Nationalist peace delegation, General Chang Chih-chung, arrived at the airport, the only thing he had to say was "Fine day, eh!" Then he went to bed with high blood pressure; he never returned to Nanking. The Nationalist press officer had already announced that another delegation, headed by Mr. Yu Yu-jen, president of the Control Yuan, would then proceed to Peking, taking with them a basket of bananas because Chairman Mao Tse-tung had not been able to obtain them since the Civil War had started. It was then announced that Mr. Yu Yu-jen could not make it to Peking because it was his birthday. The day after his birthday, it appeared that the trip was no longer necessary. The Kuomintang had turned down the Communist ultimatum, and the basket of bananas remained where it was.

The night of April 20 was noisy with gunfire. Prime Minister Ho received me the next morning and admitted that the Communists had started crossing the Yangtze River. He thought the situation might be saved with sufficient money. But supply trucks would have to choose between carrying ammunition or silver dollars to the troops, he added. The headquarters was in a state of complete chaos, and it was extremely difficult to get a straight answer as to the location of the front. On hearing the rumor that the Kuomintang government was being evacuated, I rushed to the airport just in time to photograph the exodus of the Legislative Yuan whose deputies wore their colonial hats and carried tennis rackets as though they were off on a vacation. One or two promised they would return but their voices lacked conviction. The Nationalist capital was crumbling.

Dawn of April 22 found the city in a state of nervous expectation. The end was obviously imminent. Kuomintang soldiers were also evacuating southward, complete with all their supplies and household goods. It appeared that the Communist armies had crossed the Yangtze River at points sometimes two miles wide, in wooden junks and sampans. The Kuomintang Navy showed little stomach for fight; the Air Force, even less. I was told that at the battle of Tikang, three army units known as "Chiang's Own" had revolted and defected to the enemy. At another point, the guns of a fortress had turned on its own gunboats rather than on the People's Liberation Army.

The harbor in Nanking was a one-way street heading south. Kuomintang soldiers arrived in junks with the Communists behind them. Behind me were the remnants of the government artillery. No one asked me why I was in between taking pictures. Two Navy quartermasters rushed past, chasing a pig. By the electric plant, a sentry stood, quietly watching the confusion. I wondered if any officer would think of giving him orders to evacuate or if he would still be there when the Communist troops surged onto the quays.

As Chiang's soldiers fled southward, the Communists entered from the other direction. But, during the 48 hours between the two forms of authority, the poor of Nanking, who had gone about their daily life up until then without so much as a side glance at the civil war, took full advantage of the situation. A crowd of men broke into the home of the departed Kuomintang mayor. Some talked of removing the central heating system, but that, they decided, would take too much time, strength, and skill. Instead, they ripped out doors and window frames, collected all scraps of wood, an item more valuable than gold. As long as I smiled, no one stopped me from taking pictures. The most violent plundering was reserved for the rice shop because food distribution had come almost to a halt in these last weeks. It was obvious to me that the looters were not seeking precious objects. They were stealing to provide food for their stomachs and heat for their homes. The chaos and violence were but a reflection of the state of the nation. Disorder had been reigning in the Kuomintang government for many months and little respect for it existed. I noticed that the homes and offices being looted were those of government officials who had fled in the face of the advancing People's Liberation Army.

By the evening of April 23 the flow of retreating soldiers had stopped. People were strolling quietly in the streets. The night was silent except for sporadic rifle fire. At 7 o'clock the next morning we saw our first Communist troops: a file of yellow-uniformed men walking quickly, as if they had an urgent appointment. Students and people in the neighborhood gathered about them—eager, smiling, but the soldiers paid no attention. All day, columns of these troops passed through Nanking, and I was struck by the seriousness and purpose in the eyes of these soldiers. During the night, posters and proclamations had appeared on many walls, painted by the students on the themes of the day. A group of youngsters were dancing the *yangko*, a peasant harvest dance with singing that had been revived by the Communists in their capital of Yenan. Civilians formed a Peace Preservation Corps to maintain order in the city. A few Kuomintang officers were still around, but they were now out of business and had the leisurely air of those with nothing on their mind.

Four days after "Liberation," the silk-brocade weaving looms, Nanking's main source of trade, were back in business and so was the rest of the town. It was the day of the Water Dragon Festival. The streets were gay, with herb doctors displaying their wares, vendors selling cigarettes and linen. The street-rental library was open for business and the opera was playing to an audience full of People's Army soldiers. With their straw hats and sandals, they looked more like peasants in from the fields than military men. But then, they *were* in from the fields, and obviously would know the right tilt for the hat. They also carried an extra pair of sandals strapped to their pack. And, as emergency rations, they had locusts ground with wheat grains. Their most cherished possessions seemed to be fountain pens. Many sported more than one in their shirt pockets as the symbol of their liberation from illiteracy. One of the attractions of the Communist army was classes for illiterates.

Aside from the presence of these soldiers, and the portraits of Mao Tse-tung posted everywhere, there was little evidence of the new regime. Most of the reorganization was being done in popular committees. Nanking was rapidly returning to the provincial sleepiness of pre-Kuomintang days. It was no longer Chiang Kai-shek's capital of China.

By June 10 I was back in Shanghai for the third time. By then it was in the hands of the Communist army. These young soldiers, most of them peasants, none of them administrators, were dealing for the first time with a huge complex and corrupt city. Their greatest problem was inflation. Groups of earnest students circulated in the streets, making speeches, putting up posters against the silver dollar black market, even as the money dealers were taking up their usual stand on Avenue Joffre. The sidewalks were crowded with vendors selling everything from mosquito netting to aluminum pots and pans. They were the employees of the multiple shops in Shanghai who had been paid in merchandise when their employers ran out of money.

On July 6 the Communists staged a spectacular parade against inflation. Despite the seriousness of the theme, there was an atmosphere of gaiety and release from the despair of the recent months. The sinuous dragon of Chinese tradition was conducted through the streets by the dock workers union. Students of the American Protestant University and of L'Aurore, the French Jesuit college, carried portraits of Mao Tse-tung, and the tramways, once owned by a French firm, were bright with flowers and red stars.

While the foreign population of the International Concessions was aware that its treaties and privileges probably would not be honored by the victors of the long Civil War, life went on as usual. The Americans celebrated their Independence Day on July 4 in an atmosphere of determined jollity, buoyed with rich food and drink. At the American Club, Mr. Cabot, the Consul General, made a toast and everybody lifted his glass to George Washington. At Mr. Cabot's reception, a multilingual conversation was carried on among the elegantly dressed ladies and gentlemen on the lawn, who continued their Fourth of July celebrations later at a dinner at the American Country Club, where Chinese and Jews were forbidden membership.

On July 14 the French celebrated *their* Independence Day—the first since the Liberation. Pre-Liberation, there had been a military parade in the French Concession. Now it was a series of receptions: at noon, au Petit Cercle, the club of the lower-income-bracket French, followed by another at the Cercle Sportif, the upper-income club where the French colony toasted themselves in white wine, "gimlets," and little cakes. The day was finished off with a champagne reception at the home of the consul, and finally a dance at the Cercle Sportif. The foreign colony guessed it had lost face but etiquette had not been forgotten. On July 17 the Soviet Union staged an impressive sports festival. The Russian Club in Shanghai had more than a thousand members, a great many of them White Russians who had fled their country during the revolution of 1917. Now they found themselves again under Communism, and while most other foreigners talked of going home, they knew they would have to stick it out as displaced persons.

In the meantime, the new masters were celebrating their hard-won victory. July 1, the 28th anniversary of the Communist Party, was marked by a parade as was July 7, the 12th anniversary of the Sino-Japanese War. Six days were given over to celebrating the foundation of the People's Liberation Army. But most of the Communists' efforts were directed toward restoring the economy of Shanghai. The Military Control Commission was tackling all sorts of problems, from rehabilitating singsong girls, beggars and bicycle-rickshaw drivers in more constructive jobs, to coping with the supply of rice.

The ships of the Kuomintang had established a very efficient blockade which for five months had prevented any food from being shipped in. Bad crops and floods had cut down the available sources of grain. As a result of inflation and of the food shortage, rice had become the main wage index in the city. Businessmen were using it as a standard of payment for wages.

As yet there was no code of law but only some rather vague rules regarding rents, family problems, social conflicts. Here, as in many other administrative and constitutional domains, the Communists had both to improvise and to practice face-saving. Hence, the judge in the newly established People's Court was given more to preaching than to punishing. The culprit had only to repent in a public confession, a useful method since it combined both ancient Chinese habits and the new ones of Communism.

Every day one found foreigners lined up for their exit visas. They had to advertise their departure in two newspapers so that those who stayed could collect their debts. No one knew when a boat would be able to penetrate the efficient Nationalist blockade of Shanghai's harbor. Finally, at the end of September, on three days' notice, those who wanted to leave were told to gather their belongings. The British steamer, the *General Gordon,* would take the first load to Hong Kong. After clearing my latest photographs with the Communist authorities, I was permitted to leave, thus ending my reportage on the transition of feudal China to Communistic China. Some wondered what the future would bring under the new masters. Would it be simply another dynastic upheaval in the traditional cycle, brought about by a peasant revolt, and destined to fall when the government became corrupt and degenerate? Certainly China could not shed 4000 years of history. Any revolution would be marked by tradition. In any case, the period of transition which I had witnessed served as a hinge not only between two Chinas, but between two worlds. Marx, with a conspicuous Chinese slant, had entered the Great Wall—not to replace but to supplement Confucius.

1 The impervious old man at the right is a eunuch who once served in the court of the Dowager Empress Tzu Hsi when the Imperial Court counted 400 eunuchs. They served as chamberlains to the emperors and their concubines. By 1949, only 40 eunuchs still survived and they were living in a monastery in Peking.

2 A merchant and a client greet each other in a Peking street. No anxiety mars their cordial meeting although the city is besieged by troops of the People's Liberation Army. The Kuomintang was to flee within eight days. But even on the eve of such a dramatic event, the citizens retain the calm so typical of Peking.

3 Each morning at dawn these men come to the Tai-miao Gardens in Peking to perform ritualistic exercises which serve not only to school the body, but also to discipline the mind to concentrate on matters of the spirit. In this group, there is a bank employee, a conservator of a museum, and an officer of the Kuomintang forces who does his exercises for two hours despite the steady advance of the Communist Army upon the walls of the city.

4 To a man without shelter in Hangchow, the sidewalk is his resting place. Behind him, the studio of a photographer, who also offers wedding gowns "of high style and at reasonable prices."

5 A child retained by a cord, his blind father carrying the baby and a basket for contributions—a sad but not uncommon sight on Hangchow streets in the last chaotic days of the Kuomintang regime.

6 A mother huddles her baby close to her, hoping that her sign will bring help. A refugee in the big city of Shanghai, she has written, "I am called Sun. My husband died of illness. We are strangers in this town. We have no means of existence. I am obliged to ask charity of those who have kind hearts."

7 Siesta time finds an infant asleep on a counter and his father stretched out on a bench. The store rents out mahjongg games, advertises Sword cigarettes and Champion spark plugs.

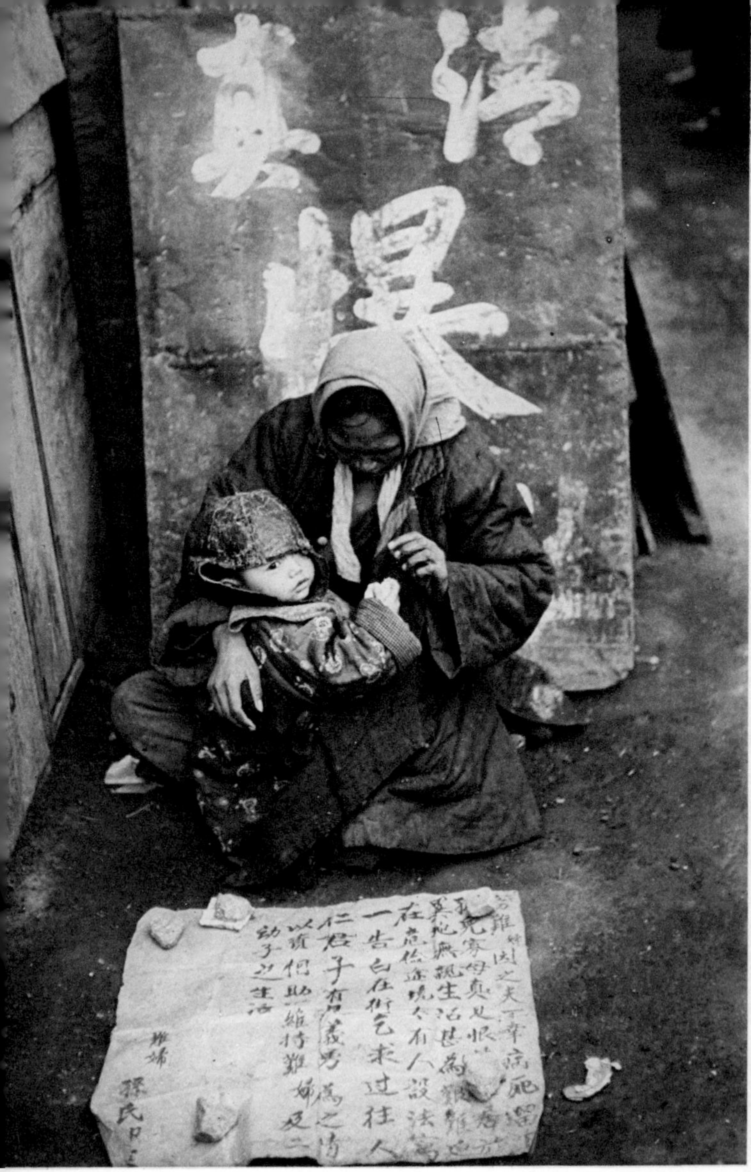

8 While his naked child sleeps, a street vendor pushes his improvised stall through the streets of Shanghai shortly before the fall of the city to the Communists.

9 Two teenage coiffeurs serve their clients in the bazaar of Nanking's Temple of Confucius. In the background a fortuneteller predicts the fate of a Kuomintang policeman.

10 Peasants rest at the foot of the ancient walls of Nanking after collecting lotus roots for fuel. In the background: Jade Mountain, and the lake where sailors received their training during the days of the Ming Emperors.

11 Youngsters help coolies push their heavy loads across one of the humpback bridges of Shanghai in hopes of receiving some payment.

12 Beggars attack a bale of cotton on Shanghai's docks along the Bund where banks and business firms conduct their prosperous trades. These women will either sell their handfuls of cotton or use it to line the quilted jackets of their families. Many were starving and freezing in this last winter of the long civil war.

13 As the value of the paper money sank, the Kuomintang decided to distribute 40 grams of gold per person. With the gold rush, in December 1948, thousands came out and waited in line for hours. The police, equipped with the remnants of the armies of the Internationl Concession, made only a gesture toward maintaining order. Ten people were crushed to death.

14 According to the newspapers posted on this billboard in Peking, the Kuomintang's armies were "advancing southward and winning important victories." But that same day, the troops of the Communist Army arrived at the gates of the city.

12

15 Mao Tse-tung's army is in control of Shanghai and the Kuomintang has fled. But the foreign diplomats and businessmen meet, as in the days past, at a garden party at the British Embassy. However, their conversation concerns the vast changes the future holds in store for them.

16 An American battleship rests at anchor amid the usual flotilla of junks on the Hwang Poo River at Shanghai. Traditionally, a British ship represented security for the foreign interests in Shanghai but in these last days of the Nationalist government, it was the United States that played the most important role.

17 As the morning mists clear over Peking, a city surrounded by Communist troops, the Kuomintang calls some 10,000 recruits, mostly shopkeepers and small businessmen, to arms. Here they receive their orders in the courtyard of the Imperial Palace.

18 A bewildered old man searches for his son as the new recruits called up by the fast-weakening Kuomintang government march off to defeat.

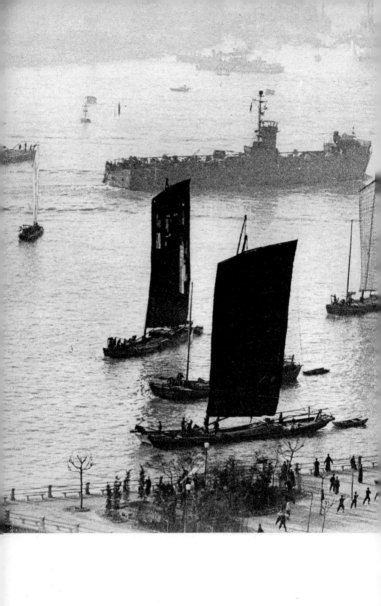

19 One of the last war lords, General Ma Hung-kouei, came to Nanking just before its fall to give his support to General Chiang Kai-shek. At the time this picture was taken, Ma Hung-kouei reigned supreme over northwest China. But shortly afterward his personal army abandoned him. On the wall behind him hang some ancient sayings, such as: "A good general should play a beautiful role in history. He should be praised for a hundred generations. He should care for his troops and also for his people."

20 The end of the last session of the Kuomintang parliament in Nanking. Shortly afterward, the Nationalist government fled as the Communists marched into the city. Only a few months before, the deputies had re-elected Chiang Kai-shek to another six-year period.

21 With their few belongings piled in a fiacre, a soldier and a boy flee the capital of Nanking just ahead of the Communist Army. In the background, the makeshift dwellings shelter the thousands of refugees of this civil war.

22 Complete with spats and umbrellas, a Kuomintang officer awaits his departure from the Shanghai station just before the final collapse of Nationalist control of the city. The Communist troops have already advanced to the far bank of the Yangtze River.

23 Peasant refugees camp out on the pavements outside the Nanking railway station. No trains have left the Nationalist capital for several days. Members of the Kuomintang government had to flee by plane.

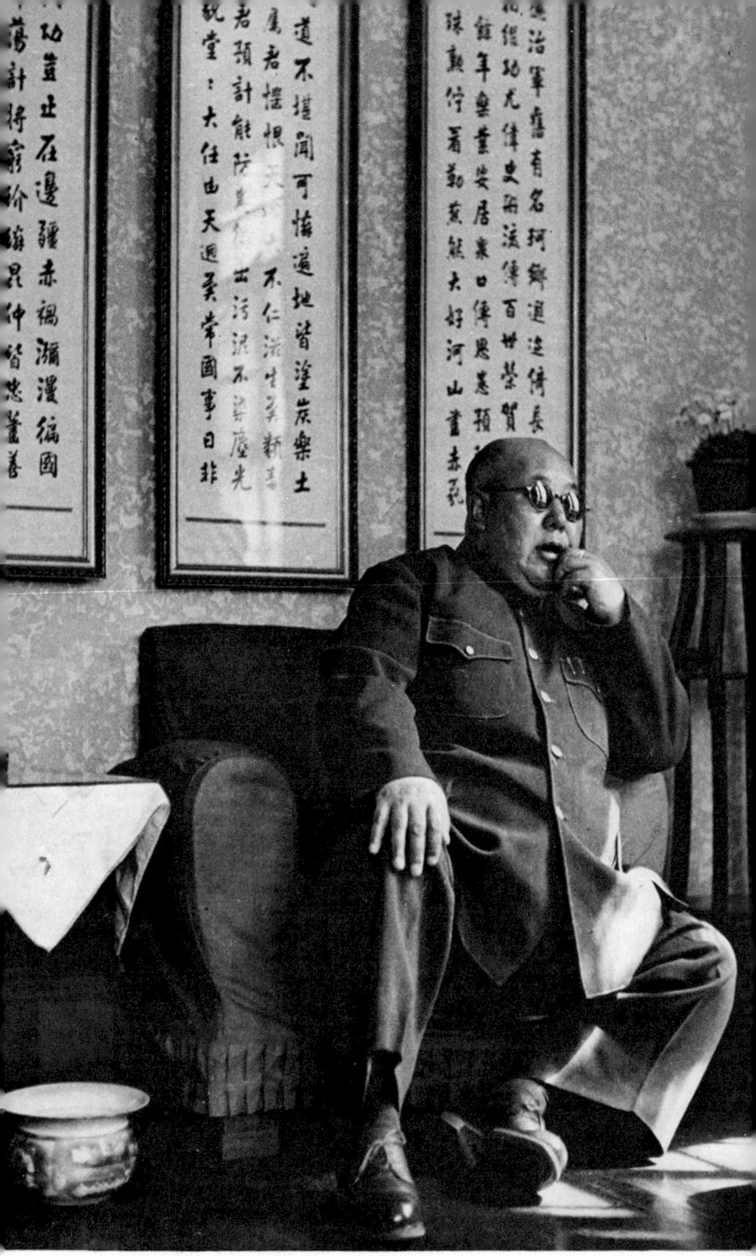

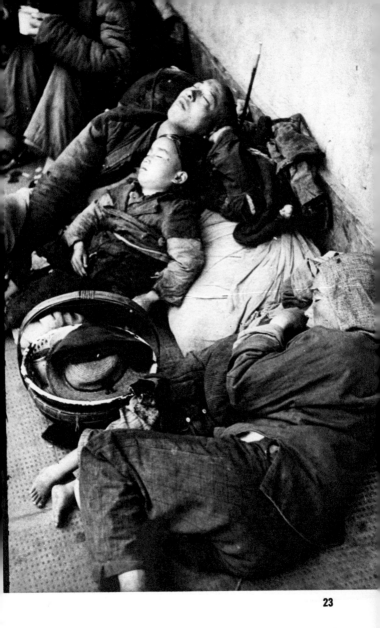

24 As law and order collapsed along with the fall of the Nationalist government in Nanking, rice stores were pillaged by those who needed food for their starving families.

25 Kuomintang officials have fled leaving Nanking without a government for two days. The streets are dangerous because of sporadic shooting, yet people stroll about, or pick up useful articles from the wreckage in the thoroughfares.

26 27 As the first soldiers of the People's Liberation Army arrive in Nanking, its citizens regard them with impassive curiosity and caution. The armies of the past lived by pillaging the land. But these troops march along chanting the three commandments: "Do not take even a needle or thread. Consider the people as your family. All that you have borrowed, you must return."

28 August 1, 1949, was a day given to celebrating the Communist conquest of Shanghai. The characters on the banner in the background read: President Mao Tse-tung.

毛澤東主席

29 During the last days of the Nationalist rule and the first days of the Communists, city streets were filled with speculators buying and selling silver dollars.

30 Students in the August 1st victory parade demonstrate against the black market as they march along Shanghai's Bund. In the background, the Soong Bank owned by Chiang Kai-shek's father-in-law.

31 In Shanghai, after the Communist victory, a well-to-do commuter carries his pocket money in bound bundles.

32 In September 1949, *The Promotion* was playing in a Shanghai theater. In this scene, Chiang Kai-shek is in a rage against his wife's brother-in-law H. H. Kung, financier and former Kuomintang Minister of Finance. The play had been written when the Nationalists were still in power, but Communists rewrote it and heightened the satire.

33 Communist soldiers at an exposition organized by the cultural service of the People's Army: the themes, the epic Long March, past misery of the peasants, and the necessity of a union between the peasantry and the army.

34 The sign above the sidewalk library in Shanghai reads: "Develop the production, make the economy prosper."

35 Shanghai youngsters devour the illustrated stories sold by wandering book vendors. Edited by the new regime, each one preaches a Confucius-cum-Communist moral.

36 Two first ladies, Madame Chou En-lai (white blouse) with Madame Sun Yat-sen (in center) widow of the 1911 revolutionary leader, listen to a speech by Communist commander, General Chen-yi, commemorating the Communist victory in Shanghai.

37 General Chen-yi, military commander of Shanghai speaks to party dignitaries at the victory celebrations of August 7, 1949. Behind him, a portrait of Chu Teh, commander-in-chief of the People's Liberation Army. Chen-yi was one of the first to join Mao Tse-tung's revolutionary party in 1921.

37

A DECADE LATER

It was ten years before I again set foot in China. Great changes had taken place. From a country torn apart by civil war, the People's Republic had built an ambitious giant. The outside world knew that the Communist rulers had extended their rule over all of mainland China including remote Tibet. In the Korean War, the Chinese "volunteer" soldiers established themselves as a fighting force to be reckoned with. But knowledge of what had happened inside the country was obtainable only through information released by the Chinese government, or in the accounts of the rare European journalists and trade-unionists granted visas.

My visa, granted by the Chinese Embassy in London, was written in Chinese characters. Having assumed that the date inscribed corresponded to the date of entry, I had not bothered to have it translated. Had I done so, I would have discovered that it was the date of expiration. Therefore, when I landed in Peking, no one was at the airport to meet me. The Deputy for Cultural Relations had assumed I had changed my mind. In the new China as in the old, the ceremonial welcome is obligatory. First the bouquet, then the speech, both enveloped in many smiles. The fact that I arrived unexpectedly and had to telephone the Ministry of Culture was embarrassing to both parties, hence a breach of Oriental etiquette. A delegation was rushed to the airport, the welcoming ritual was performed and the situation was saved. Nevertheless, I took care to start my first conference with the Third Deputy Chief of Culture with an apology concerning my ignominious arrival, before touching on the subject of my visit.

Knowing the Chinese love of rationality, their appreciation of forethought, I chose my words with precision as I explained my aims: to compare this new China to that of my first trip, then to understand the "why" behind the system and methods of the People's Republic, finally to express the "because" in visual terms. In contrast to the story of a crisis photographed in 1949, this would be an essay on China today. My work depended on contact with people and while I would listen to the official viewpoint, I would need the surprise of reality, a reality flavored neither with vinegar nor honey but one which would recount the past, the present, the failures, and the achievements. I enumerated the problems which interested me and together we charted my course on the map of China. Since the richness of reality in photography is in the element of surprise, I requested time to sniff out the atmosphere, to try to understand the nation and her peoples. But it was understood that once my itinerary was set, I could not change my mind.

From Peking, I would go to Manchuria, now called the

Northeast Provinces. This industrial region, having been stripped by the Russians in 1945, was being rehabilitated by the People's Republic with the help of the Communist Bloc. Then, down to the Sanmanchia Dam, one of several monumental projects, just off the drawing boards, destined to control the forces of the mighty Hwang-Ho (or Yellow River). From there, westward to Lanchow, gateway to the West, China's promised land. Yumen, an oil city in the Gobi Desert with something of the frenetic atmosphere of a gold-rush town, would be the first stop in the West. From Yumen to Urumchi, capital of the Sinkiang Province, would be my only trip by air because the railway lines were still under construction across that part of the Gobi. Turning east, I would visit historic Sian, then the new industrial center of Chungking where I would see the results of Communist efforts to decentralize industry from its traditional sites in Manchuria and the coastal regions. A three-day boat trip would take me through the gorges of the Yangtze River to the steel center of Wuhan, then to Nanchang, and finally to Hunan Province, Mao Tse-tung's birthplace. Shanghai and finally Peking again would complete the trip. Although I did not know it as I planned the itinerary, I would also see the first of the communes, which almost overnight were imposed on the peasantry, the most drastic agrarian revolution in the world.

"Were you able to work freely?" has been a frequent question since my return. I was given full cooperation and courtesy in the factories. But, on the streets, having a white complexion and blue eyes as well as being a photographer is almost like walking naked. Most people would ignore me, but there were times when I felt sure that the subject in my lens thought he had been chosen as an insult to the Chinese people. For instance, I learned that angry letters had been sent to Peking to denounce the foreigner who photographed laborers carrying crates suspended from poles slung across their shoulders to barges on the Yangtze River, where the steep banks demand either massive cranes or human legs. The inferiority complex of the Chinese would not admit that their industry—still in swaddling clothes—had not produced sufficent cranes to replace human beings. One of my most difficult problems was the fact that the Chinese consider candid or street photography to be an invasion of privacy. They do not like to be caught unawares. Forewarned, no one would object, but this would have hurt my sense of realism.

It was the job of my interpreter, Yu, to smooth my way. He would often draw me aside and scold: "You are becoming all red and it is very obvious. Do not be so agitated. I have told everyone that you are very polite. Be as we are. Use soft words."

Yu had been assigned to me by the Cultural Relations Ministry and obviously was responsible for my behavior if not for my understanding. He said he was generally assigned to trade union delegations and was a "greenhorn" in matters of esthetics. He was right. I enjoyed many a tussle with him over the relative merits of those square cement constructions built since the "Liberation" and the graceful pagodas of the past.

With their 4000 years of history safely behind them, the Chinese are in a position to know the meaning of time. They have learned how to caress it and how to manipulate it. Brutal violence has never been a characteristic—subtle cruelty perhaps, but not violence for its own sake. Now two stark realities have forced them to an extreme gesture: the deadlines imposed on their evolution by the world, and by their own leaping birth rate; and this to my mind is the crux of their problem. They must wrench themselves out of their fossilized economy to compete in a world where atoms and automation are the norm. And the plans drawn up for this transition from past to present are made under the shadow of a population now numbering an estimated 700,000,000 and which is increasing at the rate of 14,000,000 births per year!

In their frustration and desire to compete with the great powers of the world, the Communist Planning Committee in Peking has drawn up Five-Year development plans which, so far, might be compared to the mother who buys clothes for her children to wear five years hence, and then finds they do not fit. They are a projection of hopes for the future. Thus it was, on the eve of the Second Five-Year Plan, that China's leaders decided that a violent gesture would be needed to realize the dreams. This gesture has gone down in history as "The Great Leap Forward." It consisted of the mobilization in 1958, during my visit, of the energies of over 600,000,000 people. With this decision came the realization that China's strength was and would be in her numbers, and in their firmly controlled organization.

While such lack of freedom seems impossible to people of the Occident, one must remember that the Chinese throughout their history have always submitted to any authoritarian regime that could cope with the floods and famines which yearly devastated land and life. Now, as I was frequently told by Chinese in all walks of life, it is authority imposed in the name of and for the people, a fact that was driven in at the public meetings which I attended on communes and in factories. These play a major role in Chinese life and are like public confessions where one's moral duty to others is discussed and the benefits of participation in a given organization are extolled.

To achieve the "Great Leap Forward," Chairman Mao Tse-tung and his Planning Committee set to mobilizing the nation along military lines.

They had in their hands a huge manpower pool, mobile and interchangeable, which could be shifted from factory to field, from province to province, according to the needs of the nation. On top of this, there was the Popular Militia to serve as labor shock troops on emergencies. And the whole was supplemented and reinforced by "volunteers."

In China, everyone has to be a "volunteer" for work in fields or building roads. Thus I found little children laying sidewalks and young girls driving steam rollers, bureaucrats and intellectuals working on dams. Their production was perhaps minimal but I was told that this manual labor keeps the educated classes in contact with the peasants in contrast to the traditional pattern of past revolutions where the peasant inevitably had to bow down before the superiority of the mandarin and landlord classes.

The mobilization of so much energy gave me, at times, the impression that China had become a gigantic beehive: swarms of peasants building roads, factories, bridges, reclaiming arid fields, reforesting bare mountains.

The Ming Dam project alone demanded the labor of as many as 50,000 workers at a time, their hands replacing the heavy machinery from Russia and Czechoslovakia then in use on other projects. I saw them cut great blocks of stone by hand, watched them trudge up the steep banks carrying loads of earth in the traditional Chinese fashion with two baskets hung at either end of a pole. My guides explained with pride that 100,000 college students had "volunteered" ten to fifteen days each of work. Chou En-lai had done his bit as had many other officials. My interpreter Yu said he also had served.

While I was there, delegations from some of the minority groups arrived. They came from distant regions as though on pilgrimage to render homage to the great project. They would work with their hands for three weeks, just, as in other lands, the faithful go into retreat in a convent or monastery to contemplate their souls, and their God. But in China, God is on earth and these many thousands were constructing a sanctuary. This dam, as well as the one being built on the Hwang-Ho, can well be compared to the construction of the pyramids in Egypt in terms of labor by man's hands and sweat, but with the difference in that these dams will control water and give life, while the pyramids served as monuments to the dead.

For this reason perhaps, there was a festive air about the construction of the Ming Tombs Dam project. Huge posters either eulogized victories in production or chastised the "imperialists," particularly the Americans, for some dire deed or other. Everyone was dressed in the same austere blue cotton worker's garb during the day, but in the evening, the delegations of the National Minorities donned their colorful embroidered regional dress to dance and sing. This served as entertainment—and also served to show off the great variety and strength of China.

I returned for the inauguration on July 1 which coincided with the anniversary of the Chinese Communist Party. Speakers chanted the inevitable statistics with great pride. Thanks to the pooling of manpower, the dam had been terminated in the record time of five months and ten days. The reservoir would irrigate 250,000 *mou* of commune land: the dam would generate 240,000 kilowatts of electric power, and so on. To the peasant who suffers from drought, whose ancestors have been victims of floods, the song of such statistics has a satisfying resonance. The diplomas which General Chen-yi handed out to the best workers, the bright red banners, the songs of the delegations from distant regions all gave reason—for the moment —to the mobilization of humans.

As my interpreter explained, they can accept the backbreaking task of hacking a road out of rock by hand and will power because they have been told that the road will provide communication between formerly isolated villages. In Wuhan, my guides pointed with great pride to the Wuhan Bridge spanning the Yangtze River. Chinese engineers, they said, had constructed it where British and Japanese engineers had failed, although, they admitted, it had been accomplished thanks to the thousands of available hands rather than the "as yet" unavailable heavy machinery.

A visit to an automated factory provided an interesting comparison between their industrial ambitions and their current possibilities. The raw materials were being transported in straw baskets hung at either end of poles carried across the backs of laborers, or in hand-pulled carts and pedicabs.

The sight of this long stream of humans carrying material to be fabricated by automated machines made me ask interpreter Yu: "But what will you do with these millions of workers once automation has replaced the need of them?"

"We will organize their leisure," he said firmly.

Since the Second Five-Year Plan was drawn up to increase industrial development rather than agricultural production, Chairman Mao and his Planning Committee announced that the peasant must become a self-sufficient unit in order to give China the "Vitality of Ten Thousand Galloping Horses," a slogan which I heard and saw frequently. Among other measures, it was decided to persuade the peasants on the collectives and cooperatives to build pig-iron ovens to produce raw material for blast furnaces and for the fabrication of farm implements.

By night, the fires of thousands of native ovens made the countryside look like one vast smelting furnace. By day, the landscape crawled with humans as they swarmed into the mountains to chip coal with pick axes. If that gave out, they melted down rails, cooking utensils, and any other unattached bit of metal. According to reports announced while I was there, 11,000 native furnaces were built in that year, not only on the communes and cooperative farms, but even in Madame Sun Yat-sen's backyard. Peasants worked their own windboxes after a day out on the fields. University students smelted iron on the campuses. A year later, the ovens flickered out. It had been discovered that the material thus produced was too brittle and even farm tools snapped in two.

As I was heading back toward Peking in late August, those who guide China pushed another button, and the nation was catapulted into yet another phase of the Revolution—the communization of the land, the ultimate in organization. In a matter of a few weeks, dating from the adoption of the resolution on August 29, collective farms, peasant villages, millions of people became members of 26,500 communes.

"But," I asked a member of the commune, "isn't this a bit Leftist? Even the Russians didn't go that far with their Agrarian Towns?"

He replied with impervious sagacity: "Those who start the last arrive the first."

As I walked through the gates of the Shu Shin Commune near Peking, young peasants, rifles on their shoulders, were marching at a fast clip into the fields. As each unit halted to hoe a section, they stacked their rifles near at hand as if they expected the enemy to leap out at them from the woods. I was told that the militia drilled every day after their work in the fields, and few excuses for nonattendance were accepted. But there was a touching aspect to their militarism. While some units drilled, those who waited their turn played blind man's buff, or performed a kind of ring-around-the rosy dance. Thus no one had time to become bored or restless.

The spokesman for my welcoming committee intoned the facts and figures of the commune. It was composed of 28 villages spread over 600 square kilometers. Members were divided into Production Contingents which were, in turn, divided into Production Brigades. Each contingent elected deputies to the Commune Congress which elected the Management Committee. (It was generally understood that the Management Committee and the leaders of the Production Contingent must be members of the Communist Party.) Each village had its canteen where all the members ate, thus freeing the energies and time of many a housewife from useless duties. A sewing center to repair all the clothes freed more hands. Nurseries, kindergartens, schools, even colleges took care of the younger set. "Happy Homes" cared for the old folk. The commune had a slogan: "Organize along military lines, work as if fighting a battle, live the collective way." To further this objective, each man between the ages of sixteen and thirty, and each woman from seventeen to twenty-two years of age was supposed to serve in the Popular Militia which in turn served as shock troops on anything from building dams to reaping wheat. In line with another commune slogan, "To Each According to His Needs," salaries were not considered necessary. The "needs" ran to the already provided necessities of life, plus six to eighteen yuan per month for cigarettes and beverages.

The communes, as well as the factories, I noticed, were managed by men in their twenties or thirties who had risen up through the ranks. In Sian I met one such "self-made" peasant. He carried the official title of "Peasant Scientist" because he had created more than a hundred new seeds of corn, cotton, and wheat which had permitted him to increase the harvest on his cooperative by over two thousand "catties" of grain in three years. He was twenty-five years old, a deputy to the National Popular Congress and a member of the Communist Party. He was staying in the same hotel as I in Sian, attending a technical congress. He was dressed in the blue cotton uniform worn by all China. Two fountain pens poked up from out of his breast pocket. He looked smugly content and perhaps he had reason to be. Compared to the one- or two-room hut where he had been raised with four other children, all of whom worked the soil for a landlord, the lot of our "Peasant Scientist" was vastly improved. And he visibly felt that he owed it to the Communist regime which had given him his first chance in 1951 when he was appointed chief of a Mutual Aid team near Sian.

The most subtle form of organization in China's cities is the Inhabitants Committees, which are in fact the lower echelon, in direct line of communication with the top government and Communist Party officials in Peking.

The West District of the capital, which I visited, had 650,000 inhabitants divided up into sixteen subdivisions. To run the subdivisions there were three hundred Inhabitants Committees and another two hundred Committees for the government bureaucrats living in the West District. Each Inhabitants Committee, I learned, is composed of from four hundred to five hundred families who elect a president and a vice president plus ten deputies.

As the Deputy Director of the West explained it: "These Committees are autonomous organizations of the masses, responsible for the mobilization of manpower, the fight against illiteracy, hygiene, the repair of buildings and public security. Following the rectification movement [Big Leap Forward], the social consciousness of the masses has been very much raised. They all think work is glorious. Everyone wants to make his contribution to the country."

At the moment he was speaking those words, the people of his district were plunging into another phase of organization. Of the total labor force of 60,000, some 40,000 were being put into productive work. The rest were occupied in community housekeeping: some prepared food for the canteens, some repaired or made clothes in a sewing center. A large number took care of the babies and kindergarten-aged children "so their mothers could work with ease." The children whom I saw in their kindergartens seemed quite content with their lot while their mothers were busy manufacturing espadrilles, cardboard boxes, little plush animals, all destined for export to Hong Kong and beyond. Many of the work brigades that I saw were located, not in factories or work rooms, but in the picturesque interior courtyards of Peking where the women worked at improvised tables, rather like a sewing circle at home.

However, these Inhabitants Committees are only part of the city organization. There is also the Popular Assembly which elects the Popular Committee (47 members including the mayor and eight assistant mayors). Under this, there is the Popular Committees of Districts or communes, then the Utang or Street Committees supervising five streets. Between them, not much of a citizen's daily life is left unorganized, and few hands are unproductive, in line with the government's principle to put everyone into production. Even the aged, once the object of veneration, are put to work. Not a back, not a hand must be lost in the race against time. A common sight in city streets are the Hygiene Inspectors who by virtue of their years are elected by the Inhabitants Committees to patrol the streets. They reprimand messy housekeepers with a White Flag, and award the neat with the Red Flag of Cleanliness.

Nor are the energies of the venerable sages lost to production. In Peking's Hall of Aged Scholars, I attended a heated discussion between the wispy bearded wisemen on the relative merits of heroes. Once, these scholars were considered to be the ultimate authority on China for they and only they could read the 40,000 characters of the classical Chinese alphabet. They had been the painters, the poets, the interpreters of Confucius's philosophy. When I met them they were engaged in making a collection of biographies of heroes: maximum age limit, twenty-five years. One heretic wanted to include a twenty-six-year-old hero and a discussion was opened.

As the director explained it to me, "In this way, they contribute to the historic and cultural research for their country."

Since health is important to production, mass medical examinations are part of the social revolution, and health measures have been organized to a degree never before known in China. In one of Shanghai's fifteen districts I watched students of the city's Medical College work their way in three weeks through the heartbeats, pulse beats, blood pressures, and weights and heights of 32,000 people. A superficial examination, obviously, but one which permitted them to spot and perhaps stop the more serious diseases. The epidemics which had claimed thousands of lives in China's yesteryears would never happen again.

The Chinese have what they call "the facility to catch cold." This can mean anything from a diphtheria epidemic to a mild influenza. The methods of combating both are Draconian. As soon as I stepped off the train in Chengtu, the local greeting committee swept me off to a hotel. Politely, suavely, they told me, via interpreter Yu, that I needed to rest and that there was nothing of interest in Chengtu. Words such as these are sufficient to arouse the interest of any journalist. Against Yu's wishes, I went out for a stroll with my camera. It was quickly apparent that there was an epidemic of "the facility to catch cold" which my well-wishers had not wanted me to see, rather in the manner of the hostess who is ashamed of a messy kitchen when surprised by an unexpected visitor.

Their methods of combating it were typical of Chinese hygienic practices. At all entrance points, brigades of nurses stopped each person in order to squirt some sort of disinfectant down the throats and into all luggage. After the vaporizer, gauze masks for the mouth and pieces of cotton for the nostrils were distributed.

My lengthy train trips across the country were excellent demonstrations of the current method of making leisure productive in a didactic world. Every half hour, a rice broom was brandished under my feet. This was followed by the ballet of the tea servitors. One employee distributed the cups. A second, the tea leaves. The third man poured boiled water over the leaves. Above this activity, there was the constant blare of the loudspeaker serving up lessons on hygiene, political slogans, the latest agricultural techniques, the highest production quotas, the whole lightened by patriotic songs and classical operas.

Indeed, in this active beehive that was China 1958, every available moment was utilized. If no productive work could be done, then the propaganda machine took over, and via loudspeakers, posters, meetings, drilled the incentive to work into the national mind on a 24-hour basis. While I could not understand the speeches and had to rely on a translation, I could see the posters which were a clever blend of the direct Western art forms and the delicate tracery of Chinese tradition. The artists illustrated the two possibilities for today's citizen: an earthly paradise toward which all should be working—or descent into an Oriental Hades where monsters were destroying the nation. The monsters were the "imperialists"; the United States was pictured as being power-hungry (the U. S. Marine landing in Lebanon was the issue). Great Britain, however, was pointed out as an industrialization incentive: "Catch

Up with England in Fifteen Years" was the key slogan of the "Great Leap Forward."

To my mind the strength of Chairman Mao Tse-tung and the nucleus of Communist Party officials around him is in their knowledge of the workings and needs of the secretive Chinese mind. The messianic voice of their revolution, first heard in the Communist Soviet capital of Yenan, is now heeded over loudspeakers in trains, in city squares, and in community halls, relentlessly filling the blank silence with the dogma of the duty of brother to brother, and the benefits derived thereof. The Communist regime has created a highly moral world based on duty where the rewards are expressed by production statistics.

Even a problem such as killing off sparrows and rats was given a moral tone. Their destruction was presented as a citizen's duty toward his fellow human beings. Sparrows ate grain and rats carried disease.

Before my skeptical attitude at the idea of mass destruction of birds, Yu answered stiffly, "You are a sparrowist and not a humanist."

I regret the demise of those feathered creatures all the more that this intransigent official policy was reversed when experts discovered that the insects eaten by sparrows were multiplying since their traditional enemies had passed away. Sparrows are now permitted to flourish.

The statistics are not just for publication or foreign edification. They are quoted in meetings, in trains, on posters, in newspapers. They are the daily fare of the nation, a magic incantation which penetrates into the corners of their lives like the long sinuous dragons seen in parades.

As for the foreign visitor, listening to statistics is as necessary to the success of his visit as polished manners.

In every collective, in every factory that I visited, the routine was the same, whether it was in Wuhan or

Shanghai, Chungking or Urumchi. A receptionist would be waiting on the doorstep with a subtle smile to usher me into a vast room. A sofa covered with lace and two club chairs would be around a low table. A public relations man who doubled as a collective administrator or, in the factories, as an engineer, would present himself ceremoniously. Tea would be served, Chinese cigarettes offered. Then the public relations man would start his spiel: an account of the history of the firm before and after the "liberation"; the production figures before and after; facts concerning employees, before and after. On and on, an endless list of percentages and figures while I wistfully watched the hours of good photographic light sliding by.

Among the peasants and the workers, propaganda is spread not only through political meetings and required ideological study but also through posters and murals. In each village of a commune, there is a "Poems and Paintings" district where peasants and artists draw murals with an educational cum political theme, thus keeping Party policies constantly before the eyes of the masses. Slogans under cartoons have a moral tone: "The baptism of work and study will push the country toward a cultural revolution and bring about the individual's transformation through work."

Teams of young artists travel to distant parts of the country to paint the accomplishments of the region in fresco syle on the walls of houses. This has the double advantage of eulogizing the Communist system, and of keeping the intellectuals in contact with the masses.

Another propaganda system is that of the numbers game, a traditional Chinese device whereby a number represents a topic. Thus when Chairman Mao summons the nation to abide by "Four to Fields"—everyone knows that peasants should be: (1) holding conferences, (2) conducting sales, (3) attending lectures, and (4) eating meals in the fields in order to save time and energy for production. The "Six Guarantees" represents Minister Lin Pao's guarantee that the organization of the commune would provide for: medical care, weddings, childbirth, funerals, education, and care for the aged.

If China's present strength lies in her great manpower, her strength for the future lies outside the Great Wall, in the Gobi Desert of which the importance can be compared to that of the Far West in nineteenth-century American history.

The frenetic activity of so many millions of humans which I had seen inside the Wall is China's source of power today in her race to catch up with time. But it is in regions such as the vast Gobi in remote Sinkiang Uighur Autonomous Province that the machine is beginning to take over. Sinkiang is the current center of China's industrial development program. Claimed as part of the Chinese Empire for some 2000 years, under sporadic control for the past 50 years, and under continuous control by the Communist government since 1949, Sinkiang, I was told, is rumored to have untold wealth: oil, coal, uranium, wolfram, copper, molybdenum.

Yumen is the oil center of China. It reminded me of the "gold rush" towns in America's deserts with its row upon row of hastily constructed wooden barracks ending abruptly in the middle of the desert, and backed by a towering mountain range. Aside from these, only derricks and refineries broke the monotonous landscape.

In 1949, Yumen had a population of 4000. By 1958, it had zoomed to 80,000 people working to fulfill the slogan: "We must conquer the Gobi Desert, pierce the Chilian Mountains and have the best oil wells in China." By the time Yumen has been fully exploited, I was told, the city will not only produce petrol, but also steel, fertilizer, textiles, and tooling machinery. Such are the dreams of the future.

Deep into the Gobi Desert is Urumchi, as yet reachable only by plane or road since the railway line has not been completed. This is the capital of Sinkiang Province, and was already a bustling city back in the days of the Silk Route and Marco Polo.

It was curious to see the Chinese here. They looked strange, like foreigners.

Indeed, they are outsiders. This is the land of the Uighurs minority, a race that serves as a link between East and West for they are white and Moslem. The city is a product of many elements: Persian, Mediterranean, and Caucasian. Here are samovars and Mohammedan minarets, women in veils, and shashlik—with little Chinese Boy Scouts blowing their horns to call pedestrians to order in the streets. The popular bazaar is like the one I visited in Tashkent. The people resemble those I saw in the Middle East. They have the same love of long languid discussions concerning the affairs of the community. Down in the river, women scrub colorful rugs as they do in Iran or Greece.

The unofficial attitude toward such an un-Chinese-like atmosphere and culture is that time is on the Chinese side. Peking subtlety appreciates—for the moment—the hold of the Moslem religious leaders, the "Harounds" over the minorities, Uighurs and Hui. The faithful can be Party members, and remain Moslem. One of them, majestic in his long robe and watermelon turban, had newly returned from a pilgrimage to Mecca. He said that not only did he receive a salary from Peking for his religious duties but that the Chinese government had donated 10,000 yuan the year before for the restoration of his mosque. He also said he served as a member of the United Front—a multi-racial advisory committee on local political matters.

Millions of Chinese have emigrated from the confines of the Great Wall to this land of promise. In Urumchi's cotton, flour, and tractor factories, in her coal mines and power plants, 60 per cent of the workers are Chinese. Young university-age students from coastal provinces have come here to study in Urumchi's Institute of Foreign Languages or in the oil engineering institutions of Yumen. Collective farms are worked by demobilized Communist Army soldiers. As a result of this influx, the population of Sinkiang jumped from 4,000,000 in 1949 to over 6,000,000 today.

I was struck by the contrast between the earnest Chinese students in their austere blue uniforms striding through the streets of Urumchi with a pick over their shoulder and books under their arms, and the carefree Moslem children in their gay gowns and jackets, and embroidered skullcaps. The Chinese students were earning money toward their studies by repairing dikes along the river. The Moslems were working in a more leisurely way.

When I visited the School for National Minorities in Peking, I noted a large number of Tibetan students. Remarking my surprise, the director exclaimed: "Let them agitate in Tibet against us. It is normal since it is a feudal country. We have the youth and the future on our side."

And so it is. The old people as well as the young may retain their Moslem religion as they do in Urumchi, or revolt as they did in Tibet. But all this time the schools are educating, indoctrinating the young who see in an industrialized Communist China more opportunities than they might have under the less evolved traditions of their own cultures. Meanwhile, the Chinese are running the factories. The Chinese West is indeed the land of the future. Located as it is, on the border between East and West, its evolution might have far-reaching consequences on the peoples lying beyond it.

However, within the Great Wall, the evolution, the great and irrevocable social upheaval, has already taken place. The traditional patterns based on the supremacy of the landlord and mandarin classes have been destroyed to be replaced by a peasant-based structure invented as long ago as the first Soviet in 1927 by China's Communist leaders. The peasant, once only an illiterate serf, has come into his own as a responsible citizen, thanks in great measure to Chairman Mao Tse-tung's efforts to wipe out analphabetism. To accomplish this, he had first to cope with the problem of the Chinese alphabet—or lack of it. From the very beginnings of their civilization, the Chinese mind and culture have been formed by their written language called calligraphy, which is distinct from the spoken tongue. The classic language has 40,000 characters which transmit ideas and not sounds, which limits verbal communication since Chinese from different regions speak with vastly different tonalities. To talk, I often saw them design the characters in the palm of their hand, like deaf-mutes. This is one reason why the fountain pen is a status symbol for workers and peasants. It shows that they are literate and can communicate through writing. With the growth of newspapers and journals, a simplified written language has been built up, and a knowledge of 2000 to 3000 characters suffices for the average newspaper reader. Classes for the illiterate, held in the evening on communes and in factories, aim to teach a knowledge of 1000 characters. But unification of the country through communication is still far from accomplished, and there is talk of changing over to a phonetic alphabet with Roman characters (like ours). Such a change would indeed unite not only the Chinese but also the 18 other ethnic groups living along her southeastern, northern, and western borders. But it would also be the most revolutionary change yet wrought in their mental structure.

The prospect of a Western-style alphabet is but one of the many domains in which Communist leaders are making use of Occidental techniques. They have become expert in borrowing what is relative to their needs, and giving it a Chinese slant. In the bright up-to-date Medical Center in Wuhan, one of the busiest industrial cities, I recorded on one roll of film two medical worlds: one, up-to-date, in which a heart operation was being performed which but for the slanted eyes above the gauze masks, might have been performed in any hospital in New York; and, down the hall the ancient practice of literally studding patients with needles, carried on by equally qualified doctors. This treatment, "acupuncture" is almost as old as China herself. Based on the Buddhist beliefs concerning the balance in life and in the body of good and bad (Yin and Yang), the technique has been given scientific validity by modern Chinese doctors.

In the larger cities, such as Peking, there are modern pharmacies such as those found in the West. On the other hand, there are also pharmaceutical factories manufacturing China's traditional medicines out of herbs, grains, and many a mysterious ingredient, such as the little balls of ground deer horn, put out to dry in the sun. These are supposed to help women with cold feet and men worried about their virility.

In Shanghai, there was the contrast of earnest young medical students giving general checkups to everyone in a given district, while in a nearby park, a masseur was hard at work. His shop was a convenient bench. His customers stood to have their legs rubbed, lay down to have their backs massaged or sat for a facial treatment.

One sees in factories and fields that women work side by side with men, that women receive training as scientists and engineers, that they hold responsible positions in Party organizations.

Yet between boy and girl, man and woman, I noticed that there was still the reserve born in days past. It takes time to switch from the custom of following one's husband at a respectable ten paces behind him to walking side by side.

But it was in the many industrial and agricultural fairs that I was most conscious of the fascination with the future and the collision with the past! Peasant-invented water-wheels, wooden barrows to be pulled by hand are side by side with models of suspension bridges and models of atomic reactors. Peasants and workers were giving equal attention to past and present: examining, listening to explanations, taking notes, taking it all in with a seemingly inexhaustible thirst for knowledge and advancement.

Having rebelled so often against feudalism in their 3000 years, the Chinese peasant now sees a chance to leave serfdom behind forever. In consequence, China is in full historical renaissance, and the hands of the clock can no longer be turned back.

38 Workers in the industrial center of Chen Yang are urged to produce "still bigger, still better, more quickly, more frugally." Such slogans were typical of those posted in factories all over China during "The Great Leap Forward."

39 Political propaganda cartoons posted in a Chen Yang electrical factory chastise those who responded to Mao Tse-tung's invitation to "Let a hundred flowers bloom." One cartoon reads: Take off the mask, and behind the mask is a wolf.

40 At Peking's National Farm Implements Exhibit, a large poster depicts China catching up with Great Britain in fifteen years. To surpass the English is the ultimate aim of industry. Each coal and steel production quota is compared to those of England.

41 Near Peking's Pagoda Market, youngsters learn from this poster: "When your classes are finished you run home, but Mama will not be there, for she has gone to school." The walls of buildings across the nation are covered with such posters, each preaching a moral or lesson.

42 The "River of Sorrow," as the peasants call the 2700-mile-long Yellow River (Hwang Ho), meanders through the flats between Peking and the Sanmanchia Dam built by the Communists to provide electrical power and curb the disastrous floods which gave the river its name.

43 Built to guard the road leading to the tomb of the Ming Emperor Tchentsou, this horse seems to guard the China Eternal as well. Not far from it is the Ming Tombs Dam, product of the labor of modern China.

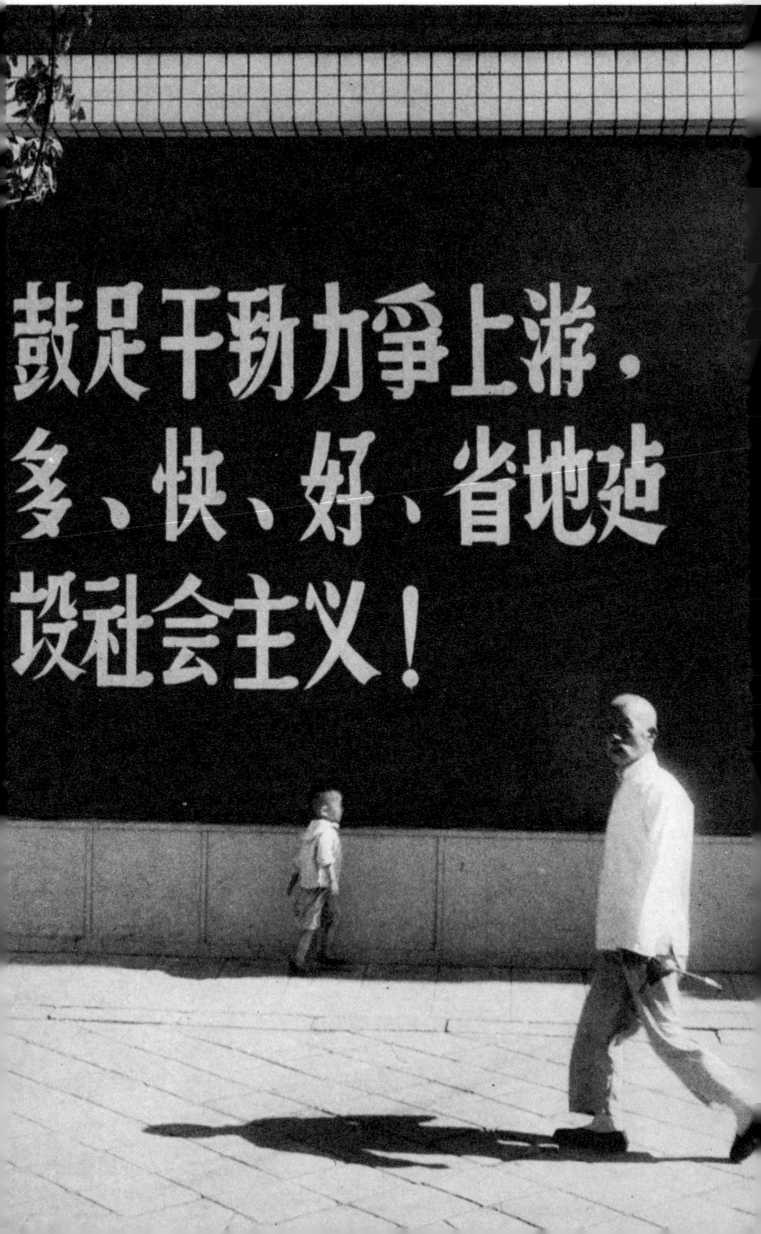
鼓足干劲力争上游，
多、快、好、省地建
设社会主义！

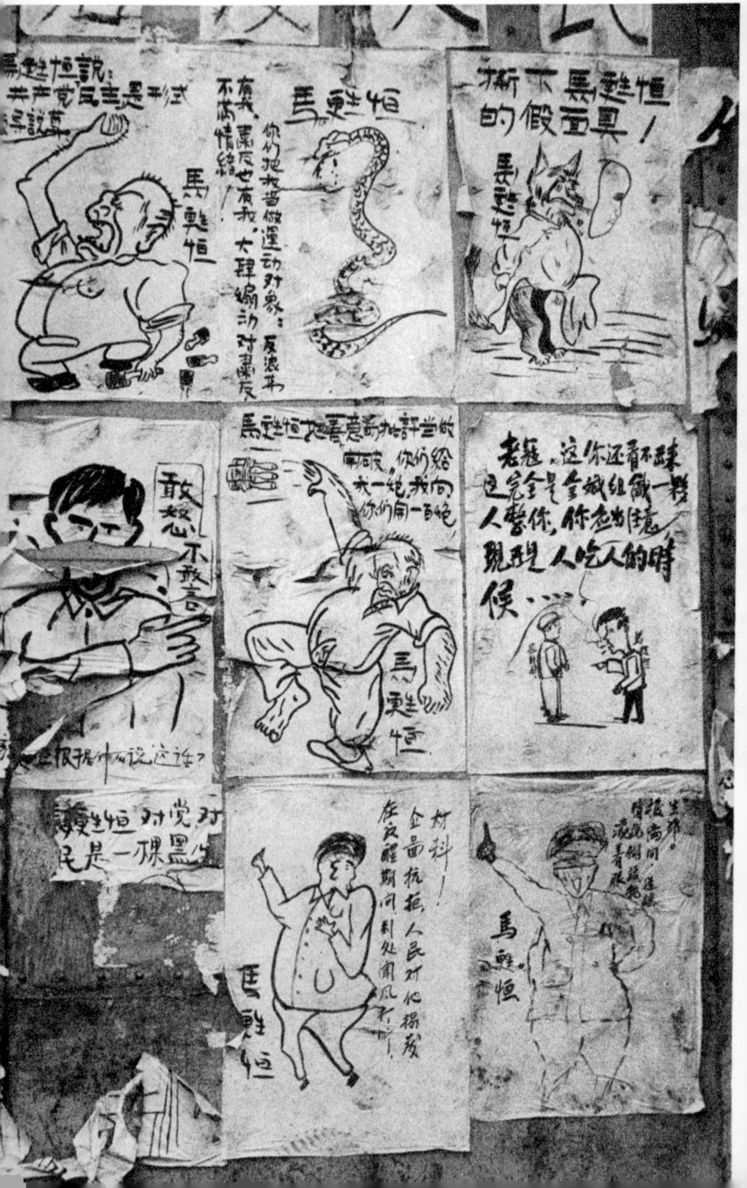
你们把我当做運动对象
敢怒不敢言

44 As a part of the drive to organize and utilize every waking hour of China's millions, this Inhabitants Committee of the Shan Shie Die Utung in Peking has organized housewives into production squads manufacturing boxes, plush animals, and espadrilles, destined mainly for export.

45 In Turfan (Sinkiang Province), shady oasis in the Gobi Desert, a mother lays down her child for a siesta. A Moslem and one of the national minorities (Uigur, Hui, Kasaks, Tatars, Shihpo, and Han), she works in the vineyards of a newly formed commune.

46 As an after-school hours project, youngsters in Sian (Sinkiang Province) pave the sidewalks of their neighborhood under the supervision of their mothers.

47 Workers pull a new lathe through the streets of Peking. Such sights are a frequently seen symptom of China's growing industrial pains.

48 On Chungking's docks, men unload the barges by hand; mechanized equipment had not yet been installed. Several citizens wrote letters of protest to Peking when Cartier-Bresson took this picture, claiming that his action was an insult to the Chinese people.

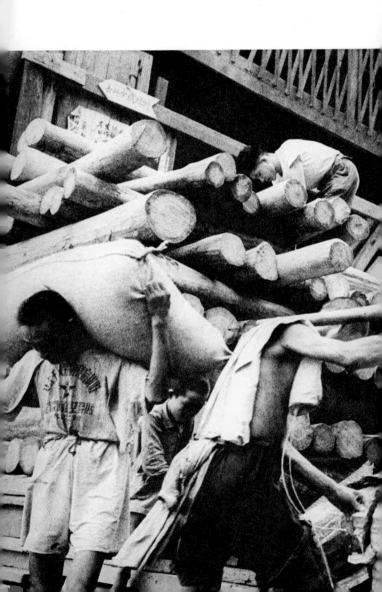

49 During "The Great Leap Forward" peasants were encouraged to construct their own smelting ovens. Here, peasants work their wind boxes on the Shiu Shin Commune near Peking. Every half hour these ovens smelted about one hundred pounds of iron used by the peasants to make their own farm tools. But the homemade metal proved too brittle and the tools snapped in two. Such labor was done after the normal work day spent in the fields or rice paddies.

50 Thousands of volunteers, including top functionaries and shopkeepers, put their shoulders to the task of building the Ming Tombs Dam near Peking in a record time of five months and ten days. The regime publicized the presence of the scholars and government employees (up to the level of Chou En-lai) as evidence that all shared the lot of the peasant in Communist China in contrast to the wide gap between classes in pre-revolutionary days. City folk were strongly urged to volunteer for this project.

51 Steel-mill construction workers in the industrial complex of Wuhan finish work on an automatic blast furnace with the aid of the kind of baskets used by coolies for many centuries. Caught with a shortage of heavy construction machinery, the Communist regime takes full advantage of its greatest asset, a man-power pool six million strong.

52 Women, traditionally considered inferior to men, have a more equal place in society thanks to their share in the long war against Japan. Although physical contact in public is unknown, boys and girls, like these two in Shanghai, may be seen on lovers' promenades.

53 Building up cadres of engineers and scientists is a major aim of the Communist regime. This student is studying in the Peking University library.

54 Visitors take notes on a peasant invention at Peking's National Farm Implements Exhibit. The government encourages such inventions in order to make the peasants feel a part of the new order.

55 An older professor corrects his class papers by the lake in the newly built King Chan Park in Peking.

56 Shanghai laborers play a Sunday game of checkers in one of the city's nineteen "cultural" clubs.

57 Typographer searches for a "character" at newspaper printing plant in Peking. Readers must know 2000 to 3000 "characters." Illiterates aim for knowledge of 1000, and cultured people know 20,000 of the 40,000 "characters" in the classic language.

58 In Peking's Hall of Aged Scholars, a heated argument on relative merits of young heroes whose biographies are being compiled as a contribution to the new order.

59 Workers of the Fou Choun (Northeast Province) synthetic oil plant at a production quota meeting.

60 Pigtailed students stride to class in the Chen Yang Engineering School.

61 An oil worker in Yumen, in the Gobi Desert, beats her drum as she leads a delegation to administration headquarters to announce their production quotas.

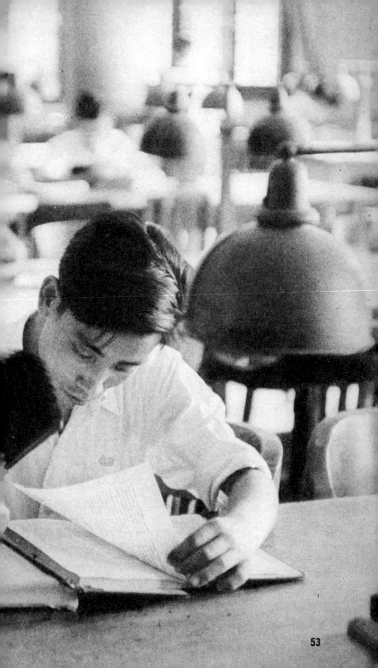

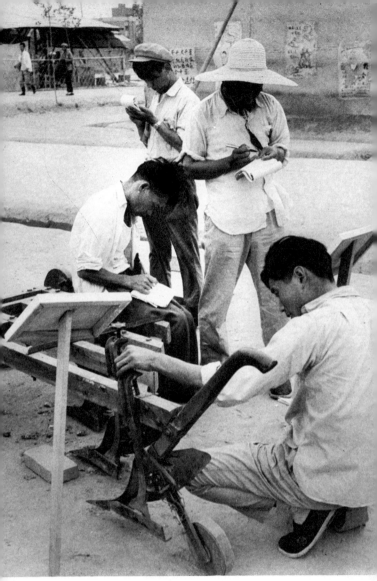

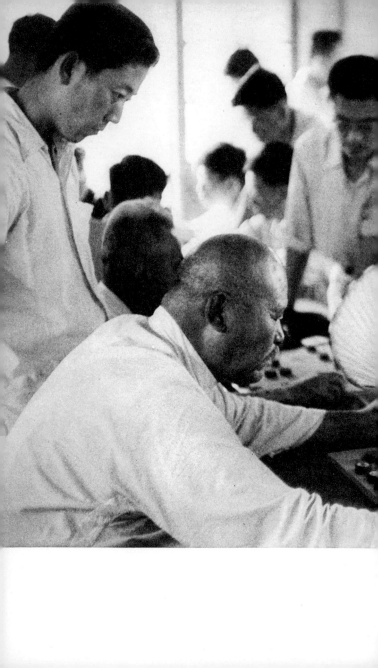

62 Armed with a gay parasol and a shovel, two young ladies of Chen Yang set off for their stint as volunteers on a community construction project.

63 This Pioneer (Girl Scout) is charged with seeing that the people of Urumchi (capital of Sinkiang Province) use pedestrian crossings, and fly swatters on the region's pestiferous flies.

64 The extermination of China's four scourges—flies, mosquitoes, rats, and sparrows—is the theme of this exhibit in Peking, illustrated by a rat made of ratskins.

65 A male nurse disenfects all who enter Chengtu in an effort to halt an epidemic. Fearful of their well-known "facility to catch cold," the Chinese use Draconian methods to combat it.

66 Peking prison inmates rehearse a traditional sword dance. According to the director, the prisoners (two-thirds are political prisoners) are reformed by work and study.

67 Work-study programs are an integral part of Chinese university life. Here an engineering student of Chen Yang works a lathe.

68 One of the Communist regime's major efforts, the Sanmanchia Dam, is destined to provide one million kilowatts of electricity for three provinces as well as to curb the treacherous waters of the Yellow River.

高山低头 河水让路

69 Eager visitors hear about the technological progress made since the Communists came into power at the Bridge and Railway Exhibit in Peking.

70-71 Students of Peking University plunge into a swampy bog in order to make themselves a swimming pool rather than wait for unavailable machinery.

72 Symbol of greater ease in the future, the refrigerator draws delighted visitors to Peking's Palace of culture.

73 Closed-circuit broadcast permits Chinese to view both themselves and TV for the first time at an exhibit in Peking's Palace of Culture.

74 In Wuhan's heavy tooling factory, a worker regulates his milling machine. Construction of this factory started in 1956. According to its director, 80 percent of the machinery is Chinese-made and 20 per cent, Czech and East German-made.

75 With the intense desire to learn that is so typical of the Chinese, visitors measure and take notes on new tools exhibited at Peking's Agricultural College.

76 An oil-tank train rumbles its way across the vast Gobi Desert. Still under construction, this railway line will link China to the Soviet Union for the first time.

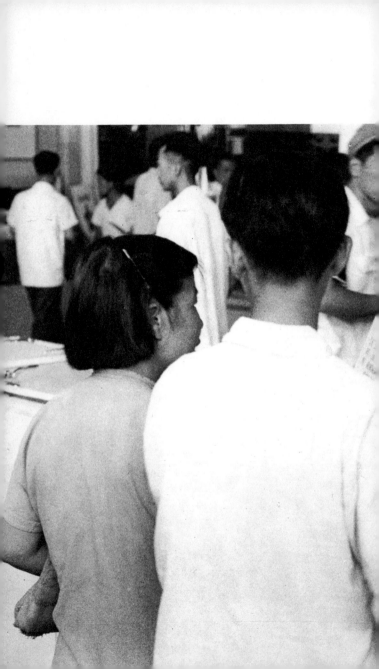

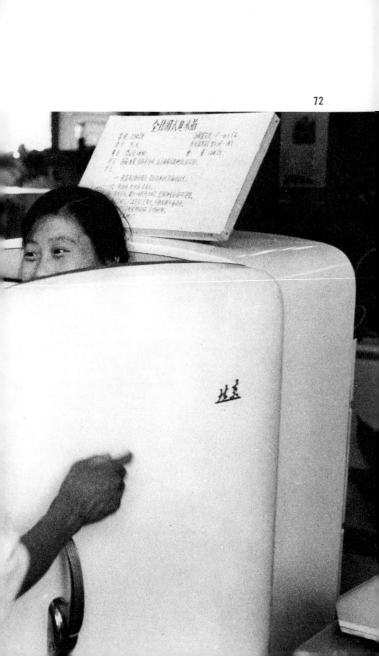

77 Schoolboys rest after their daily drill on the Shiu Shin Commune near Peking. Sons of peasants, they form a militia trained in the handling of guns, hand grenades, and such enemy agents as might be dropped from planes. On the wall, the slogan: "Everybody loves to work."

78 A unit of the People's Militia awaits their turn at the daily morning drill. In the background, Peking's Tien An Men Palace where the country's leaders stand to review patriotic parades.

79 At ease beside the arms of her unit, a woman member of the People's Militia of Peking catches up on official reading matter before beginning her daily drill.

80 Art is considered to be "an arm of combat" by communist China's leaders. This poster, painted by a student of Peking's Art Institute depicts Uncle Sam as a treacherous serpent during the Lebanese crisis.

81 A young Chinese shouts violent slogans during an anti-American demonstration in Peking. Such demonstrations provide an outlet for resentment against the difficulties of daily life which might be directed elsewhere.

82 To celebrate the tenth anniversary of the new order in China, a gigantic parade marched through Peking. As young athletes, Buddhist monks, and Catholic nuns danced or marched, a symbolic flock of peace doves was released to fly into the sky. But the refractory dove in this picture seems content to watch the girls.

83 New China's athletes celebrate her 10th birthday under the stern eyes of communism's founding fathers.

84 Exhibitions, both agricultural and industrial, provide the Chinese masses with a vision of future comfort which helps them endure the hardships of the present. This mother and child standing at the entrance to Peking's Industrial Exhibit have glimpsed the result of plans projected for the time the child enters adolescence.

85 A face out of China's eternal past peers impassively at an exhibition in Peking's Park of Culture where the "Bridge and Railway Exhibit, scale models of the future are on display. Prior to the "liberation" by the Communist Army, this old man had probably already seen three revolutions.

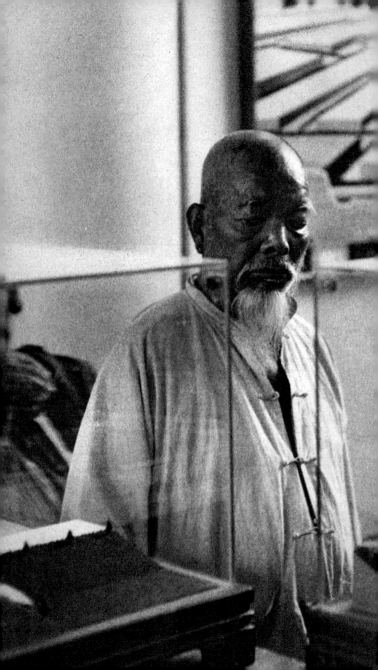

From Myth to History

The roots of China penetrate deep into the past, so deep that we cannot date the origin of the Chinese civilization. We think it to be about 4000 years old, but the people and their lives are obscured by a thick mist of legends which did not clear away until a millennium later when the structure of this ancient civilization emerges.

At that time it was centered in the rich loess terrain of the middle valley of the Yellow River in the north of China where the absence of a primeval forest made it possible for a neolithic people to start a poor agriculture of millet and wheat with crude tools. The loess soil provided homes as well. Caves, warm in winter and cool in summer, were easily hollowed out of the cliffs, and were readily defendable.

Those farmers who were the most able mobilizers of the manpower needed to irrigate, cultivate, harvest, and defend the fields of grain, became the rulers. In legends, they had the stature of semigods who were masters of the people and of their providence.

Among the famous mythical rulers was Fu Hsi, supposedly the inventor of pictorial writing, the calendar and medical instruments; Shen Nung (the Divine Cultivator) was reputed to be the father of agriculture. Then came the reign of Huang-ti, the Yellow Emperor (2698 B.C.), the inventor of the compass and the combat chariot. The Empress, his wife, was said to have started breeding silkworms.

With Yao, the Golden Age of China began. The people of that time believed their land to be "Chung-k'o" or "country of the center of the earth," a phrase which governs their thinking today as it did in the past. Man was attached to his morsel of earth, to his mulberry tree (source of silkworm), and to the tombs of his ancestors. A poem was born at that time which has lived throughout China's 4000 years of history:

> *When the sun rises, I work,*
> *When the sun sets, I rest.*
> *What use is imperial power to me?*

The Golden Age came to an end when the philosopher-king, Shun, successor to Yao, handed his Empire over to his "virtuous minister" Yu. Yu became strong, as had no other ruler, through his successful efforts to expand and develop irrigation. He was the founder of the first dynasty, the Hsia Dynasty (2200–1700 B.C.) about which we know more through legend than fact.

The sophisticated five-hundred-year-long civilization of the Shang Dynasty (1600–1100 B.C.) provides us with our first reliable historic knowledge. These people developed a pictographic form of writing most of which can be read today. A social structure developed based on a peasant or subject labor force; this pattern lasted, with minor variations, until Sun Yat-sen attempted to introduce the principle of democracy 3000 years later. The owners or rulers of both peasants and land were a minority. These men with leisure time to keep up their skill in hunting and war also created a form of writing, and invented an agricultural calendar for planting. Thus was created both a feudal class of warriors and a cultivated gentry who became heads of the powerful landowning class. Small walled towns surrounded by the well-cultivated fields that supported them began to appear, forerunners of the agricultural pattern which still dominates China.

Confucius Says . . .

The Chou Dynasty (1050–256 B.C.) was a troubled period when the many feudal lords disputed the authority of the kings. But progress was made in irrigation techniques and canal construction. A state administration was created, born of the need to regulate irrigation projects and control graneries around which walled cities were built. Such cities became self-contained units, then banded together to form separate kingdoms and, eventually, a unified imperial state such as the Chou Dynasty attempted to found. This dynasty however foundered as a result of constant strife among the feudal lords. From this period came three of China's greatest philosophers: Confucius, his predecessor Lao-tzu, and his successor Mencius. All were contemporaries of Socrates and Plato. After Lao-tzu and Confucius died religions based on their teachings were organized.

The system based on Confucius had neither clergy, hierarchy nor theology, hence could scarcely be called a religion in the Western sense. The Master avoided discussions of metaphysical problems with his disciples (a practice characteristic of China's intellectuals even today). Instead he demanded that they conform to a moral code, the Five Relationships: obedience to feudal overlords, of sons to fathers, of younger brothers to older brothers, of wives to husbands, and loyalty between friends. To become a bureaucrat, it was necessary to know the rules of Confucius, preserved in the Analects.

Mencius was more concerned with economic matters. He supported feudal law, but held that the upper classes should care for the welfare of the lower classes. If not, he warned, the oppressed would revolt.

Lao-tzu's mystic philosophy called "Tao" or the Way, was based on thoughts of kindness, humility, and brotherly love. After his death, in 666 A.D., Taoism was recognized as an organized religion with a large priesthood.

The philosophic religious ideas of Lao-tzu and Confucius developed simultaneously in Chinese history until Buddhism was introduced from India in 60 A.D. During the Sung (960–1280 A.D.) and the Ming (1368–1644 A.D.) dynasties neo-Confucianism—Confucianism tinged with Buddhism—prevailed.

Unification and Oppression . . .

When the Chou Dynasty began to collapse under the destructive effect of feudal wars, Sh'h Huang-ti completed the feudal conquests, unified the country, and put an end to anarchy in 221 B.C. He took the name of Ch'in Sh'h-Huang-ti, First Emperor of China and of the Ch'in Dynasty (although it went no further than his son).

The fighting ended, Huang-ti created a new order of society by decreeing the end of serfdom and feudalism. Peasants were made owners of their own land and paid taxes directly to the state. But in freeing this large pool of manpower, Huang-ti was faced with the problem of providing work and pay for those who had no land. He decided to expand the Great Wall until it measured some 2000 miles. This Herculean feat was accomplished through the forced labor of many thousands, who also constructed a network of roads necessary for the military defense of the Empire.

In an effort to destroy the last vestiges of feudalism, Huang-ti massacred a large number of intellectuals and ordered their books and papers burned so as to exterminate what he called "The Dangerous Thought."

But so oppressive was Huang-ti's rule, that a rebellion broke out after his death, while his son, the Second Emperor, was on the throne, and the dynasty fell.

The anti-Ch'in revolt in 206 B.C. was led by a minor official of the restive Huai region, Liu Pang, a man on the perimeter of the gentry class but sufficiently cognizant of the workings of the state to make use of Sh'h Huang-ti's administrative system and unification. He founded the Han Dynasty (206 B.C.–A.D. 220). Confucianism was decreed the official doctrine, and the new Emperor initiated an examination system for civil servants based on knowledge of the philosopher's sayings. It was a prosperous period and one of military expansion under the Martial Emperor, Wu-ti, who created a Central Asian colonial empire which extended to Russian Turkistan, built up China's hold over South Manchuria, Korea, and Indochina. The Central Asian conquests gave the Han control of much of the famed "Silk Road." Thus citizens of the Roman Empire were able to trade with China.

With the fall of the Han came four centuries of complete disorder. Nomads from the north invaded, plundered, and seized land. Within the Great Wall, struggle raged between the Three Kingdoms, the Chin and the

Northern and Southern Dynasties. Nevertheless, with the entry of Buddhist missionaries from India, Chinese art was enriched by colossal stone and bronze statues of Buddha.

The T'ang Dynasty came into being in A.D. 618. The same year marked the completion of the Grand Canal which linked the Yangtze Valley in the south to the Hwango-Ho or Yellow River Valley in the north. It was to be the nation's main artery for the next fourteen centuries. The T'ang period was one of prosperity, of great poetry, and of expansion—as far as India—into the greatest Empire yet known to China. This unified and peaceful dynasty declined under the blows of invading tribes from the steppes—Thais, Tibetans, and Uighurs—and collapsed in A.D. 906 to give way to yet another period of anarchy which ended in the rise of the Sung Dynasty in A.D. 960 and an artistic renaissance. Ornate pagodas were built. Paintings, complex in composition and color, were created on silken scrolls. The magnetic compass was developed as well as an inoculation against smallpox, seven hundred years before the British discovered vaccination.

Off the Steppes . . .

Then, the hordes of Genghis Khan rode out of the steppes. The Mongolian conqueror had invented an almost infallible system of warfare based on cavalry that lived off the land, that outrode, outsurrounded, and overwhelmed its less mobile enemy—a system not unlike that used by the Red Army in their fight against Chiang Kai-shek's forces. Known as the Yuan Dynasty (1260–1386), the Khan Emperors ruled over an immense Empire which stretched from the Pacific to the Danube. The fourth Mongolian Emperor, Kublai Khan, chose Peking as his capital. The thriving commerce, and the splendor of

Peking and Hangchow, ancient capital of the Sung, were described in the accounts of Marco Polo, a Venetian trader who became a functionary in the administration. But, despite Kublai Khan's cultural efforts, the Chinese never accepted the Mongols, considering them to be barbaric and uncultivated. The Yuan Empire was so vast that it began to collapse from its own weight. Peking could not control the loyalties of Mongol armies in lands as distant as Southern Russia. Thus, the Yuan Dynasty fell in a series of civil wars.

Again, it was a Chinese of rather humble origins who defeated the Mongols and founded the Ming Dynasty (1368–1644). A later Ming Emperor created the plan of the Imperial City in Peking, and in its heart, the beautiful Forbidden City. Traditional culture was esteemed, but there was a flowering of new knowledge in science and medicine as well as the creation of the porcelain statues, bowls, and cups so prized today. Two thousand scholars produced an encyclopedia containing China's collected wisdom.

The Beginning of the End . . .

The Ming Dynasty, as with all China's dynasties, grew weak and corrupt. Unable to defend her borders against invaders from Manchuria and Mongolia, it fell when the Manchus captured Peking in 1644. Thus was started yet another dynastic cycle, that of the Ch'ing, which was to be China's last. For a time it prospered but then, as had always happened with other dynasties, widespread corruption and imperial inefficiency brought defeat in 1911— this time under the impetus of the revolution started by Sun Yat-sen, a movement which was to terminate in the Chinese People's Republic. Only the future will tell if this revolution has broken the seemingly inevitable 4000-year-old dynastic cycle pattern of history.

There are several theories concerning the reasons behind the dynastic pattern in Chinese history. One stresses the declining power of each imperial family over the centuries due to dissipation and neglect of duties, leading to a rise in power of the nomads on China's borders, or of the downtrodden peasants. Another is based on the dependence of the rulers of the mandarin class, a bureaucratic group which had grown in numbers and importance to preside over the interests of the state. This mandarin or "scholar-gentry" class circulated freely throughout the country. They served not only as a link between the Imperial Court and local administrations, but also as a link between dynasties, preserving the old systems despite the new masters who, through lack of administrative knowledge, were forced to turn to them. Naturally, the mandarins were eager to preserve their monopoly, and discouraged any variation on the theme. Thus each dynasty was fated from the beginning to follow the same cycle: revolution, agrarian affluence, maintenance of the status quo, diminishing returns as the supply, restricted by the system, failed to meet the demand, and finally another agrarian revolution which destroyed the state but not the system, kept in well-oiled working order by the mandarins.

The peasant-gentry schism was maintained by the long apprenticeship required to learn the classic written language. China is and was a land of many dialects, and the main means of communication was (and is) in the 40,000 "characters" each of which stands for a word. Only men of leisure and money could permit themselves this privilege; therefore approximately nine out of every ten Chinese remained illiterate.

The intent to maintain the status quo, the worship of past cultures, plus the practice of ancestor worship (belief that the living owe a debt to the dead), kept progress down to a minimum and self-satisfaction up to a maximum degree . . . until traders from the West came to inflict defeat and humiliation on the nation as a whole, and to open their eyes to their own weaknesses.

China: The Open Door . . .

Until the nineteenth century, the Chinese knew little of what went on outside their country. They lived in the security of their isolation, and in their long and brilliant past. Arrogant by ignorance, they had no respect for Westerners, calling them "The Big Noses," "The Hairy Ones," or "The Demons." In the eighteenth century, only the port of Canton offered trading facilities.

Friction between the Chinese and the British grew because of the opium trade. This illegal trade expanded from 4000 chests to 18,000 in forty years. When the Imperial Court ordered the seizure of 20,000 chests, the British waged the Opium War (1839–42). They overwhelmed the Chinese, and dictated the humiliating Treaty of Nanking in which Hong Kong was ceded to the British and five new ports to exterior commerce were opened. In a supplementary treaty, the British were granted "the most favored nation" treatment regarding trade. France, Russia, Germany, Belgium, and Sweden hastened to grab their "concessions"—pieces of territory over which each foreign power ruled. From the peak of their pride, the Chinese fell to the lowest level of humiliation and all conditions imposed by the West were granted: extraterritoriality, equal tariffs on national and foreign-made goods which prevented the Chinese from protecting their own production. After further disputes and defeats, new treaties gave the victorious European Powers the right to sail up the Yangtze River and the right to have a foreign inspector in the customs service. Finally, they gained the right to import opium. "China," said Sun Yat-sen, "is a colony, exploited by all and ignored by everyone." Even certain of the Chinese cooperated with the foreigners, as agents or supervisors, and a new milieu was created called *compradores.*

In the south, resentment against a government that could not protect the nation from foreign invasion grew into the T'ai-p'ing Rebellion (1851). It lasted ten years, the rebels gaining control of half of China including Nanking. But the Manchu Emperor, with the help of the armed forces of the foreign traders, crushed it in 1864, just as the rebels were preparing to seize Peking. The war dead came to 30,000,000.

The West continued to nibble away at the Empire: Britain in Burma and Nepal, the French in Annam, Indochina; Russia built up railways in Manchuria and established a naval base. In a war over a conflict of interests in Korea, Japan defeated China, annexed Korea and Taiwan, and, in flagrant disregard for Chinese laws, launched a campaign of deliberate demoralization and exploitation by establishing houses of prostitution and opium dens.

In 1900 there was another violent anti-foreigner revolt, this time in the north of China. It was staged by the Boxers, a Secret Society whose name translates something like "The Fists of Righteous Harmony"; they believed in the protection of magic rites against the weapons of the foreign devils. After massacring the Chinese Christians whom they considered the dupes of foreigners they attacked the legations. When they threatened the safety of the legations, a military expedition of the Western Powers (including the United States and Japan) defeated the rebels and then looted Peking in a manner as brutal as that of the Boxers.

The partition of China at this time was prevented partly by the quarrels between the irate foreign powers and to a degree by the "Open Door" policy proposed by United States Secretary of State John Hay by which every nation had equal rights of trade and agreed not to dismember

China. A major effort to strengthen the nation was made by two Chinese leaders—K'ang Yu-wei and Sun Yat-sen. After the Sino-Japanese War of 1894, K'ang Yu-wei launched a reform movement with the support of the young emperor. This short period is known as "The Hundred Days' Reform" (1898). Unfortunately, the empress dowager ordered a return to the status quo.

By 1908 revolt flamed again under the leadership of Sun Yat-sen. This Cantonese had founded the Kuomintang, a political party based on three principles: "Nationalism, Democracy, and the People's Livelihood." He protested the humiliating position of his country vis-à-vis the foreign powers, and the overwhelming misery of the people. In 1911 the Imperial regime collapsed under the onslaught of a successful revolution. The child Emperor, Pu-yi, was forced to abdicate and he retreated into the European Concession of Tientsin.

Sun Yat-sen was elected President of the Republic, but the power of the army was still in the hands of Yuan Shih-kai, Prime Minister under the Manchus, and Sun finally had to step down. Yuan attempted to make himself Emperor—in traditional style—but the provincial generals refused to support him. Yuan's actions had discredited the Republic, and, throughout China, the power passed to men who commanded local armies. For the next ten years, China's history was to be a confused struggle between these competing warlords. Each profited by collecting the taxes, in his own region, often well in advance. In 1920, the peasants of one province had paid taxes for the year 2000— eighty years in advance. At that time, they were already paying 45 per cent of their income in land taxes and surtaxes. If the peasant lacked sufficient money to "lend" it to the warlord, his future depended on the humor of the tax collector—his house might be burned, his daughter raped, his buffalo stolen and he himself shot. In the cities, little boys and young children and young women were sold into jobs which bound them as slaves to factories for as long as five years, working twelve to thirteen hours daily. Some slept beneath their machines. None were permitted to leave the guarded premises without permission.

Sun Yat-sen and his Kuomintang Party organized a Revolutionary Government in Canton, and until his death from cancer in 1925, he continued to work for a united modern China. He accepted the offer of cooperation from the newly formed Communist Party. Founded in 1921 as the Kungch'antang (Share Production Party), by, among others, Mao Tse-tung, it too advocated a unified China, free of the onus of her colonial status. Many Chinese Communists joined the Kuomintang while secretly maintaining ties with the Party. Soviet advisers, including Adolf Joffe and Michael Borodin, were sent to reorganize the Kuomintang and train the army. During the period of Kuomintang-Communist collaboration, the Communists held important posts in the Kuomintang organization. In 1926, Mao Tse-tung became Secretary of the Peasants Committee for the Kuomintang, and founded the same year the All China Peasant's Union. Chou En-lai was Secretary of the famed Whangpo Military Academy, Chiang Kai-shek's officer's training school.

On Sun Yat-sen's death, Chiang Kai-shek, a disciple of Sun and the Kuomintang's leading general, took over the leadership. The Canton Revolutionary Government, Communists and Nationalists, decided to fight the authority of the warlords. In 1926 Chiang led the "Northern Expedition." From Canton, his troops took Nanking with little opposition from the local armies. Shanghai fell to them thanks to the General Strike and uprising of the workers organized by Chou En-lai. By 1927 Peking was also under Kuomintang control.

Having accomplished his mission to unseat the warlords, Chiang Kai-shek signed an alliance with the "Tai-pan," the European and American directors of foreign interests. At the same time, he turned against his Communist Party collaborators and Russian advisers. Many Communists were arrested and executed and the Civil War was on. Before it was finished, the executions of Communists, alone, amounted to two or three thousand, the number of war dead, on both sides, to several million.

Under the leadership of Mao Tse-tung and Chu Teh, the Communists withdrew into the mountains of Kiangsi Province in the center of China. In November 1927, the first Soviet government was set up by election in Tsalin, defended by the newly formed units of the first Peasant and Worker's Army. The Communists got rid of the rich landlords and practiced land distribution to the poor. Unable to match the power of the Kuomintang Army, the Peasant Army resorted to guerrilla warfare.

In the meantime, Chiang Kai-shek's regime in Nanking had been recognized by all the powers of the world and his prestige was high. His armies made four unsuccessful attempts to defeat the Communists in Kiangsi. The fifth time, Chiang tried a new strategy: a circle of blockhouses was built to surround and starve them out. Facing disaster, the Communists had to retreat or be wiped out. In 1934, almost 100,000 of them broke through the surrounding forces and started an exodus called the "Long March."

When they reached their destination of Shensi Province in the north, a year later, they had marched on foot more than 6000 miles. Only about 20,000 survived the arduous trek and the frequent attacks by the Kuomintang armies. But this mass migration was to prove the biggest propaganda tour in history, for the Communists used their contact with some 200,000,000 Chinese to sow the seeds of Communism—explaining the agrarian revolution, arming peasants, leaving "cadres" behind to train them, confiscating the property of the "traitors" (officials, rich landlords, and tax collectors) and distributing their land and goods.

On reaching Shensi, they set up their capital in Yenan where the only office space available was in caves.

Japan, profiting from the Civil War in China, had occupied the rich provinces of Manchuria ever since 1931, ruling through the puppet Emperor, Pu-yi, China's last Manchu Emperor. On July 7, 1937, they attacked Peking and occupied much of the north. A few weeks later, Japanese troops attacked Shanghai and in December 1937, they attacked and took the Nationalist capital of Nanking, sacking, looting, and killing for nearly two weeks.

After the occupation of Manchuria, Generalissimo Chiang Kai-shek was under popular pressure to wage war with Japan and to cease wasting the nation's energies in a Civil War rather than avenging the occupation of Manchuria. But it took a military mutiny staged by one of his own commanders, the "Young Marshal," Chang Hsueh-liang of the Northeastern Army in Sian to force him to his decision.

The Japanese stopped their advance by 1940 after they had occupied Manchuria, the coastal regions and the lower Yangtze Valley. But it was not until their defeat by the Allied powers in September 1945 that China was free of the Japanese menace.

No sooner was this war ended than the Civil War recommenced despite the efforts of General George C. Marshall to effect a truce and a coalition government. The Kuomintang Army, well equipped and trained, was confident of a quick victory over the ragged Communist troops. In February 1947, Yenan had fallen to the Nationalists but to their astonishment they had not won the war. In August, the tide turned when Ling Pao, the Communist Army's greatest general, won his first victory in Manchuria. The following year, the Communists controlled northern

China, including Yenan, and, in October 1948, they began the siege of Peking and Tientsin, the last northern cities under Nationalist control. By February 1949, Mao Tse-tung once again entered the city where he had been the assistant to the conservator of the Peking University Library in 1917.

During the preceding year, the Nationalist government had been growing weaker and weaker, destroyed by interior corruption, the Japanese, and Civil Wars. No effort was made to help the peasantry or industrialize. Discontent was rife. Money lost its value, and hordes of frantic city people rushed to buy rice and gold. In April 1949 the Communist Army conquered Nanking; in May, Shanghai. Chiang Kai-shek resigned and the defeated Nationalist armies fled to Taiwan. In October 1949, Mao Tse-tung proclaimed the People's Republic of China.

The First Thirteen Years . . .

China, in 1949, was ravaged and exhausted by twelve years of civil strife and war. Its transportation system and industry were but a "modern fringe stitched along the hem of the ancient garment." Some 80 per cent of the population was agrarian, yet only 11 per cent of the land was arable—and that worn thin by centuries of intensive cultivation.

To govern the new "people's democratic state," Chinese Communist leaders set up two interlocking organizations: the Party and the Government. At the top: the Politburo, composed of the Chairman of the People's Republic (formerly Mao Tse-tung, now Liu Chao-chi), the Premier (Chou En-lai) and five others. Premier Chou En-lai heads the Cabinet. Provincial and regional Assemblies elect 1200 deputies to the National People's Congress.

The Chinese Communist Party now has 14,000,000

members, making it the largest in the world. Its structure resembles a pyramid. At the base, the "cadres" (Party members) carry out government orders. At the top: the National Party Congress and the Politburo. In between, Party members hold key jobs in every level of the government organization.

Agrarian socialization started with land redistribution to the peasants. Mutual Aid Teams were organized to share manpower, draft animals and tools. By 1954, Producers Cooperatives were established in order to pool arable land. Between 1955 and 1957, some 96 per cent of all the peasants were collectivized. In 1958 came the "Great Leap Forward" and the transformation of 740,000 collectives into 26,500 communes. Both movements were born of the failure to industrialize to the extent envisaged by the State Planning Commission in its First Five-Year Plan.

Industrial socialization started in 1951 with "thought reform" movements, such as the San Fan movement against the Three Evils: corruption, waste, bureaucracy. By 1952, private enterprise had been reduced by 40 per cent. By 1955, state control of private commerce and property was total. Businessmen had been persuaded by heavy doses of ideology plus raised taxes and increased red tape to let the state take over. In turn, they were retained as managers and paid (until 1962) compensation for the expropriation of their property.

The First Five-Year Plan, drawn up in 1953, aimed to double industrial output in five years. By the end of 1957, the decentralization of industry was well under way. China was able to produce its first trucks and automobiles, to export complete sets of cotton, textile, plywood, and paper-making machinery to her neighbors. If the quality was not of the highest, the satisfaction of China's leaders was enormous at having produced anything at all.

But, at the same time, the lack of balance in planning was beginning to hamper progress. Too little capital had been invested in agriculture to produce necessities of life like sugar, edible oil, cloth, vegetables, chemical fertilizer. Equally there were shortages in construction steel, timber, coal, and bamboo.

On February 27, 1957, Chairman Mao uttered the now famous phrase, "Let one hundred flowers bloom and let all the schools of thought face each other." Directed to the often dissident groups of artists, writers, and scholars, it was an invitation to blow off steam in a time of grim austerity. The intellectuals responded with such a flood of criticism that, by June 8, Chairman Mao had had enough, and the guillotine fell. Those who had criticized were called "rightists" and duly punished either by imprisonment or by being sent to work on the land.

Today, under the guidance of the omnipotent "cadres," discussion of government and party policies is permitted as part of the Communist technique of thought "education." Thus, if a wage cut is decreed in Peking for factory workers, the "cadres" in each factory summon workers to "discussion, criticism, and education" meetings. The result: the "cadres" can announce to Peking that the workers have "volunteered" to take the wage cut.

In the face of the production crisis, Chairman Mao and his State Planning Commission examined their resources and decided to further mobilize their greatest force—the peasants. It came to their attention that some 500,000,000 people were not as gainfully employed as they might be.

Peasants, thanks to nature's cycle, only worked two hundred days per year. Wives and mothers were spending their time in unproductive (for the state) housework and child care. In all, this "free" time added up to billions of work days. The organization of the peasants, through the "Great Leap Forward," and afterward, the commune, took but a short time in 1958, thanks to the structure which had been built up over the years. Each collective farm was now to become a self-supporting unit, even to producing its own steel for farm implements. When peasants were not hoeing or harvesting the fields, they were keeping the blast furnaces alight, building irrigation systems, hacking roads out of rock, planting trees, making their own cement, their own farm implements and, at the same time, providing 75 per cent of the raw materials needed for factories as well as feeding the nation. On some communes, dormitories replaced homes. Communal mess halls were set up in the fields to save time. The workday was twelve hours long plus two hours at night of ideological study.

The goal: completion of the Second Five-Year Plan in three years. Peking triumphantly blared out the results of the mass mobilization. Production quotas, they said, had increased at least 100 per cent in all domains.

But in the summer of 1959, nationwide food shortages forced Premier Chou En-lai to announce the truth. The blame was put on the natural calamities (floods and drought) which had affected one-third of the farmland. From Peking came an embarrassed scaling down of statistics. Industrial production was but 65 per cent higher and agricultural production but 33 per cent higher.

In the summer of 1959, clothes and food rationing were decreed. Meat and fish were for the four national holidays only. The amount of cloth per person was but two and a half feet per year.

Faced with the fatigue and passive resistance of the peasant millions, China's leaders reconsidered the structure of the commune. The workday was limited to ten hours plus two hours of ideological studies. Husbands and wives were permitted to have their own room, as well as bicycles, watches, radios, furniture, small farm implements, and a few domestic animals. Payment for work was no longer "according to need," but "according to ability and work." Small plots of land were turned over to individuals who were permitted to eat or sell the produce on the "free market" where prices doubled and tripled those of the state markets. To stimulate production, the state's share in the income of the commune was sharply reduced and three-fourths of the income was redistributed to the members. On the eve of the Third Five-Year Plan, efforts were shifted from industrial to agricultural development. The nation would have to catch its breath before continuing the race to catch up with the atom age.

Nevertheless, despite the impression China gives of leaping to great heights only to fall halfway back in defeat, an impressive economic growth has taken place in the past thirteen years. According to Western statisticians, steel production is thirteen times higher than the peak year of 1943: electricity is five times higher than the prewar level, and twelve times higher than the 1949 level. There is four to five times more coal mined today than in the best pre-Communist period. Grain crops have doubled those of 1936, the peak year. Operating railways and highway mileage have tripled since 1949. Airline and telephone lines link together all parts of the country, including those reached before only by foot. China is now the world's second-ranking producer of tin and the ranking producer of tungsten.

And, out of a nation of illiterate peasants, the Communist regime is pushing ahead to create a nation of literate technicians. In 1946, approximately 80 per cent were illiterate. Today, Peking claims that three-fourths of the people can read and write. From primary schools to universities, there are over 100,000,000 students, four times the level of 1949. Out of higher education institutions come 100,000 graduates annually, compared to a few tens of thousands in 1947. Over one fourth are engineers. As a result of the works study system, any one of them can put a hand to a lathe as well as draw up plans for dams and bridges.

Peking's Institute of Atomic Energy has a reactor and cyclotron in operation, a gift of Soviet Russia. The new Chinese University of Science and Technology opened its doors in 1958 and offers courses in applied physics and related sciences. Students work three months and study eight months in each year of the four-year course. The aim is to have a factory in each of the thirteen departments to manufacture research equipment. The Academy of Science is currently opening branches throughout the provinces and autonomous regions. According to Peking, 50 per cent of the university and technical institute students are sons and daughters of peasants and the citizens of China's future.

Barbara Brakeley Miller

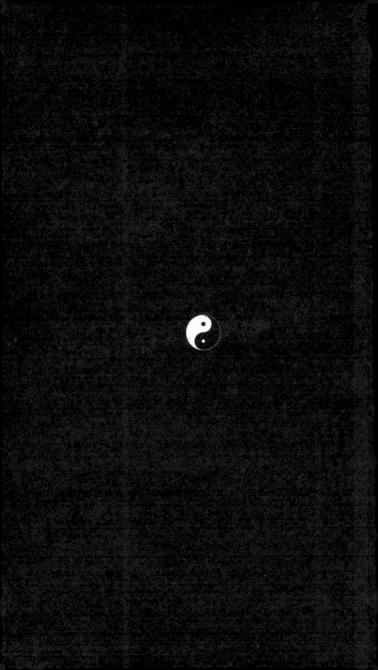